Inspirations

A collection of commentaries and quotations to promote school improvement

Tim Brighouse
and David Woods

Published by Network Continuum Education
The Tower Building, 11 York Road
London SE1 7NX

www.networkcontinuum.co.uk
www.continuumbooks.com

An imprint of The Continuum International Publishing Group Ltd

First published 2006
© Tim Brighouse and David Woods 2006

ISBN-13: 978 1 85539 222 9
ISBN-10:   1 85539 222 4

Managing editor: Judith Oppenheimer
Layout and cover design by: Marc Maynard, MM design
Illustrations by: Bentley Holland & Partners

Printed in Great Britain by Ashford Colour Press Ltd, Gosport

What is a quotation? It is a saying or piece of writing that strikes people as so true or memorable that they quote it (or allude to it) in speech or writing.

The Oxford Dictionary of Modern Quotations
Preface

He wrapped himself in quotations – as a beggar would enfold himself in the purple of emperors.

Rudyard Kipling
Many Inventions

A book that furnishes no quotations is no book – it is a play thing.

Thomas Love Peacock

Contents

Acknowledgements

We would like to thank Judith Oppenheimer for the enormous care she has taken to check the text and quotations, and for her suggestions regarding the presentation of the text.

Particular thanks are also due to Gina Henderson, who prepared the original typescript of this book and patiently dealt with many changes afterwards.

We wish also to acknowledge the schools in Birmingham and London who have provided ideas for the 'butterflies'.

Introduction

This little book is intended for busy headteachers, teachers, heads of departments and subject co-ordinators.

We know very few teachers – and fewer schools – who haven't found a quotation useful from time to time to either improve or reinforce a message. Along with story and anecdote they are the stock-in-trade of teachers keen to 'unlock the minds and open the shut chambers of the hearts' of the students they are anxious should enjoy and be energetic about their learning.

We have even come across one school whose idiosyncratic headteacher and staff decided at the beginning of one school year to introduce a 'Quid for a Quote' scheme which led to the school's environment being transformed by over a thousand framed quotations each 'donated' by a student. 'Of course we have a member of the support staff whose duties include leading the visual environment of the school. And she suggested the idea. Said it would help her task enormously,' declared the head as he explained what had so changed the visual appearance of the school.

He then described how he, the two deputies and each year head of Years 7 to 10 had led 'Assemblies' vividly illustrated by their own preference for particular quotations and why they mattered to them. Then the students in each tutor group were asked – reinforced by its being the first English homework of term – to go home and collect five quotations which the whole family valued. 'We said five because we calculated at least one would be OK,' smiled the head. Then the deal was that if one was chosen it would be properly framed and hung in the school – different subject and year areas using different themes.

But the nice touch was the promise that in return for the framed quotation each student would be given a pound to be used for a charity of the family's choice. 'We didn't insist on their donation,' declared the head, with a slight raise of the eyebrow.

This story about quotations illustrates a feature of this book – namely, that it contains 'butterflies'. Butterflies derive from the 'butterfly effect' of chaos theory, which suggests that the whirring of a butterfly's wings in the Amazonian rainforest can affect the climate elsewhere – causing tornadoes, for example, in North America. So 'butterflies' in management terms, within organizations like schools, are small ideas which, if implemented, can have a disproportionate effect. Preferably they need to be what David Hargreaves has called 'high leverage'. That's to say, that for very little effort they have high impact – as opposed to the reverse, namely interventions which require enormous effort for very little outcome!

So this book contains quotations and butterflies. It trades in ideas too. But in writing it we are deeply conscious of the importance of context. What may work in one school or one situation at a certain time doesn't work at another time and in a different place. This issue – of context and culture – explains why in second headships some school leaders fail. They forget that, like good teachers, they should have learned the lesson of unpredictability when something that has worked nine times out of ten then inexplicably fails.

Nevertheless this book attempts to do something else. We unashamedly and unforgivably write in a fairly prescriptive way a few pieces that precede the clutch of quotations and butterflies. It's because (between us) we've seen so many schools, and occasionally shaken our heads in disbelief that the obvious things haven't been done or applied consistently.

The groupings – of General Education; Leadership and Management; Teaching; School Improvement and Evaluation; and most importantly, Learning – seem to us to be useful pegs on which to hang our various coats and hats.

Enjoy.

Tim Brighouse and David Woods

Chapter 1

General education

> It is important that students bring a certain ragamuffin barefoot irreverence to their studies. They are not here to worship what is known, but to question it.
>
> Jacob Bronowski
> *The Ascent of Man*

We all have acknowledged or unacknowledged purposes in mind when we are involved in education and teaching. For the art and music teacher in education the main driver may include the hope that they encounter and develop young artists and musicians who may excel or be fulfilled by their own emerging skill, flair and competence. They hope that even where the aptitude to perform remains stubbornly locked, the student will appreciate the art form in a way that enriches their life. For others, for example in the primary sector, it is likely that the teacher's enjoyment comes from seeing pupils' emerging and growing competence in the three Rs – in the purest form of 'reading', 'reckoning' and 'wroughting' with 'wrighting'. To this they would now presumably add establishing pupil competence in what would be described as e-learning or a basic 'literacy' in using the learning and communication technologies. In doing this, primary teachers understand that across a broad range of knowledge they are laying the essential foundations of the child's learning before handing the baton on to secondary colleagues who try to build in adolescence on what's been achieved in childhood. Even before this, in the pre-school years, educators are working to optimize the very earliest environments in which the infant is nurtured. There are of course long arguments among those involved in the education of each of the stages of a child's development about the best way of achieving their ends. So for example in early years education in the UK we tend to press for achievement in the three Rs as soon as we can. In some other cultures there is a much stronger belief in and emphasis on 'constructive play' and sensitive observation of the child's development. The Steiner approach would be an example of that extended well into the years of childhood.

It appears to be a disagreement not about ends but rather of means. And yet it may be worse than that. Disagreement about means may hide differences about purposes too. Is for example our main aim to produce individuals who are able and sufficiently competent to take their economic role in life, contributing as adults to the wealth-creating activity of a society either as employer, or as employee, or as a freelance or solo agent? Others would see the main purpose as one of individual and collective social justice. So for them the main purpose is to create the capacity in the individual to argue a case which is just and to support those who have not been educated to have sufficient voice to do that. The latter is close to being a supporter of education in its own right and the former to being a supporter of education as an economic instrument.

It's a very unfair and simplistic set of general propositions but the columns opposite seek to represent the one approach or the other.

For novelists it is a battle between the Gradgrind of Dickens on the one hand, and on the other Muriel Spark's Miss Brodie:

Instrumental	Education in its own right
Intelligence is predictable	Intelligence is multifaceted and capable of being developed
Subject knowledge is more important than experience	Basic skills are a necessary precursor of an individual's being able to argue a case which is just
Successful schooling is a passport to a good job	Successful schooling is an entitlement to a good life
You only get one chance to learn and it's now	Learning is lifelong
Teacher-focused	Learner-focused
Children are motivated by what education will lead to as a passport in life	Children are motivated by learning something that thrills them and makes them want to engage in the activity more
Provides answers	Asks questions
Education is a competitive race where there are winners and losers	Education is a collaborative activity where everyone can be successful in the end
Education is about providing answers	Education is about asking questions
People will know their place	People will create their place

'To me education is a leading out of what is already there in the pupil's soul.'

The H.G. Wells quotation we cite ('Human history becomes more and more a race between education and catastrophe') is capable of many interpretations. If applied to society as a whole it's a case for investing more; if applied to the individual, it's a spur to action to help the young either to escape from being another family victim of the cycle of deprivation or, if they are from a well-off and supportive background, to avoid their falling into it.

Your reaction to the polarization set out in the table above is not that it's one or the other, but it's both. Nevertheless you will probably not give both sides equal weight.

There is currently much discussion in England about the Every Child Matters debate, which brings together the social care and education agendas. The government have set five fairly uncontroversial outcomes for their new unified policy for children.

Children should:

Be healthy, which involves the physical, mental, emotional and sexual well-being ... (in short all the intentions of the Healthy Schools campaign).

Stay safe, which involves waging a continual battle inside and outside school against bullying, antisocial behaviour, drugs and crime.

Enjoy and achieve, which involves being ready to take advantage of learning, attending school and enjoying it, and working in a school environment clearly committed to the highest educational standards of provision and outcome.

Make a positive contribution, which involves engaging in decision making and supporting their community and environment (that is, what we now call student voice); engaging in law-abiding and positive behaviour in and out of school; developing positive relationships; developing self-confidence and successfully dealing with life's changes and challenges; and developing enterprising behaviour.

Achieve economic well-being, which involves engaging in work, further education and training on leaving school and throughout life; being ready for employment; and living in a decent household free from low income in a sustainable community environment.

It can be seen that in their aims the government seek to encourage both traditions.

Most of those in schools will find resonance in the following reflection of Frank McCourt at the end of his teaching career as he pursues an imaginary conversation with his students:

> This is where the teacher turns serious and asks the Big Question. What is education, anyway? What are we doing in this school? You can say you're trying to graduate so that you can go to college and prepare for a career. But, fellow students, it's more than that. I've had to ask myself what the hell I'm doing in the classroom. I've worked out an equation for myself. On the left hand side of the blackboard I print a capital 'F', on the right hand side another capital 'F'. I draw an arrow from the left to the right, from FEAR to FREEDOM.
>
> I don't think anyone achieves complete freedom, but what I'm trying to do with you is drive fear into a corner.[1]

Finally by way of introduction, education for us has a political implication. The Bishop of London in 1803 said that it was 'safest for the church and the state that the lower classes should remain in that state of ignorance into which God had originally placed them'. And when in 1870 the first Education Act was passed Robert Lowe was famously heard to say after the passage of a recent Reform Act extending the vote, 'We must educate our masters'. Though not too thoroughly apparently, for he was also quoted as saying that 'the education of the poor should be just sufficient to give them that sense of awe for higher education that the leaders of the nation demand'.

---

[1] F. McCourt, *Teacher Man*, Fourth Estate (2005).

In the uncertain world of today, in a less deferential and more participative society and in an age which can be described as the 'Information, Technological and Creative Age' our young people need more. One's view of education and its importance will be influenced by not one religion but many, not one race but many, not one language but many. We need youngsters prepared to live out Rawls, the American philosopher's, advocacy of the 'fact of reasonable pluralism'. In short, I may believe I am right about how to live the good life and I may believe that you are wrong. And I shall argue my case as fiercely and certainly as I can but I will always respect your position even though I believe you to be profoundly mistaken.[2]

Of course one's interpretation of what limits to put on the values we have to live by at the time and about which we may seek to argue, will vary from time to time and society to society. It is, however, hard to see how any form of democracy can flourish without education doing its work, a reflection which, if accepted, has enormous implications for the speed of fostering democracy in the developing countries of Asia and Africa, and perhaps for the connection made with communities in those continents by the schools of the UK.

---

[2] Quoted in J. Leese, *Personalities and Power in English Education*, Arnold (1950).

Quotations

Education is the lure of the transcendent – that which we seem is not what we are for we could always be other. Education is the openness to a future that is beyond all futures. Education is the protest against present forms that they may be reformed and transformed. Education is the consciousness that we live in time, pulled by the inexorable otherness ... To interpret the changingness of human life as 'learning' and to rein in destiny by 'objectives' is a paltry response to humankind's participation in the divine or eternal.

D. Heubner
'Religious Metaphors in the Language of Education'

A child educated only at school is an uneducated child.

George Santayana
Quoted in *The International Education Quotations Encyclopaedia*

Until Education has done far more work than it has had an opportunity of doing, you cannot have society organised on the basis of justice; for this reason that there will always be a strain … between what is due to a man in view of his humanity with all his powers and capabilities and what is due to him at the moment as a member of society, with all his faculties still undeveloped, with many of his tastes warped, with his powers largely crushed. Are you going to treat a man as what he is, or as what he might be? Morality requires, I think, that you should treat him as what he might be, as what he has it in him to become … and business requires that you should treat him as what he is; you cannot get rid of that strain except by raising what he is to the level of what he might be. That is the whole work of education. Give him the full development of his powers; and there will no longer be that conflict between the claim of the man as he is and the claim of the man as he might become. And so you can have no justice at the basis of your social life until education has done its full work. And then again, you can have no real freedom, because until a man's whole personality has developed, he cannot be free in his own life … And you cannot have political freedom any more than you can have moral freedom until people's powers are developed, for the simple reason that over and over again we find that men with a cause which is ... just are unable to state it in the way which might enable it to prevail ... There exists a mental form of slavery which is as real as any economic form. We are pledged to destroy it ... If you want human liberty you must have educated people.

William Temple
Citizen and Churchman

It's fine to celebrate success but it is more important to heed the lessons of failure.

Bill Gates
Quoted in *The Hutchinson Dictionary of Business Quotations*

Soap and education are not as sudden as a massacre, but they are more deadly in the long run.

Mark Twain

Education is an ornament in prosperity and a refuge in adversity.

Aristotle

Nothing in education is more astonishing than the amount of ignorance it accumulates in the form of inert facts.

Henry Brook Adams
The Education of Henry Adams

The only effective method of education is to be an example.

Albert Einstein
The World as I See It

The aim of education is the knowledge not of facts but of values.

William Ralph Inge
The Oxford Dictionary of Phrase, Saying, and Quotation

Education is what survives when what has been learnt has been forgotten.

B.F. Skinner
New Scientist, 21 May 1964

A genius! I have practised fourteen hours a day and now they call me a genius.

Pablo Sarasate, violinist

The young Michelangelo took to the Pope, who was to employ him on the building of the Dome of St Peter's and on the painting of the Sistine Chapel, a reference which said 'The bearer of these presents is Michelangelo, the sculptor. His nature is such that he has to be drawn out by kindness and encouragement but if he be treated well and love shown to him he will accomplish things that will make the whole world wonder.'

Alec Clegg

We pass through this world but once. Few tragedies can be more extensive than the structuring of life, few injustices deeper than the denial of an opportunity to strive or even to hope, by a limit imposed from without but falsely identified as lying within.

Stephen Jay Gould
The Mismeasure of Man

… make them discontented with the evil circumstances which surround them. There are those who say that we are educating children above their station. That is true, and if you return me I shall do my utmost to get them such knowledge and such discipline as will make them thoroughly discontented, not indeed with that state of life into which it shall please God to call them, but with the evil state into which anarchy and monopoly has forced them, so that by their own organised and disciplined effort they may live fuller lives than you have been able to live, in a more beautiful world than you have had to toil in.

Revd Stuart Headlam
London School Board Election Address (1888)

There's nothing permanent except change.

Heraclitus

The empires of the future are the empires of the mind.

Winston S. Churchill
Onwards to Victory
Speech at Harvard University, 6 September 1943

We are what we repeatedly do. Excellence, then, is not an act, but a habit.

Aristotle

We receive three educations, one from our parents, one from our school masters, and one from the world. The third contradicts all that the first two teach us.

Montesquieu
Quoted in *The International Education Quotations Encyclopaedia*

Only the educated are free.

Epicetus
Quoted in *Grey's Essential Miscellany for Teachers*

Hope is definitely not the same thing as optimism. It is not the conviction that something will turn out well, but the certainty that something makes sense, regardless of how it turns out. It is hope, above all, that gives us strength to live and to continually try new things, even in challenging conditions.

Vaclav Havel
Disturbing the Peace

We must become the change we want to see in the world.

Mohandas K. Gandhi

- ➤

Mankind owes to Children the best it has to give.
Their life is fragile.
If they are to have a tomorrow
Their needs must be met today.
Many things can wait, but not the children.
Now is the time that their bones are being formed.
Their blood composed, and their senses developed.
We cannot answer their 'tomorrows'.
Their name is 'today'.

Gabriela Mistral
Selected Poems

◄ -

No man can reveal to you aught but that which
already lies half asleep in the dawning of your
knowledge. The teacher who walks in the
shadow of the temple, among his followers,
gives not of his wisdom, but of his faith and his
lovingness. If he is indeed wise he does not bid
you enter the house of his wisdom, but rather
leads you to the threshold of your own mind.

Kahlil Gibran
The Prophet

There are two lasting bequests we can give our children: one is roots. The other is wings.

Hodding Carter, Jr
A Collection of Poems

Our deepest fear is not that we are inadequate. Our deepest fear is that we are powerful beyond measure. It is our light, not our darkness, that most frightens us. We ask ourselves, who am I to be brilliant, gorgeous, talented and fabulous? Actually, who are you not to be? You are a child of God. Your playing small does not serve the world. There is nothing enlightened about shrinking so that other people will not feel insecure around you. We are born to make manifest in the glory of God that is within us. It is not just in some of us, it is in everyone, and as we let our own light shine, we unconsciously give other people permission to do the same. As we are liberated from our own fear, our presence automatically liberates others.

Nelson Mandela
Long Walk to Freedom

The school will be a huge old house full of spacious rooms decorated in vibrant colours. Just because it is a learning institution doesn't mean there have to be small grey classrooms in rows containing scratched grey desks in lines. No gum will festoon the undersides of tables because there will be bins; and pupils won't be afraid to use them because rules like 'detention if caught with gum' would be recognised as counterproductive. People will see that chewing does not actually hinder learning.

There will be a huge library open to all pupils at any time. There will be bean bags and sofas to sit on and read comfortably. These won't be vandalised because once pupils are treated as intelligent human beings they will behave so.

I must admit to my share of graffiti on the science lab gas taps as sixty students have gathered (and have spent half an hour being herded) around a desk to watch water boil. If the teacher had simply recognised that we were people with brains she would have realised that we all knew what water looks like while boiling. She could have said 'When water boils …' and got on with the lesson, instead of driving me to the frustration it takes to write 'Get me out of this f***ing dump' in pencil, not even caring about the possibility of her wrath if caught. (Fortunately my comment went unnoticed amongst all the other clumsily worded cries for salvation that decorated the physics lab.)

My ideal school will produce real people who respect and accommodate others instead of having prejudices. No one will have unfair power over them and so they will never abuse their power over others as so many adults do today. They will have been treated fairly and celebrated as individuals; not discriminated against just because they are powerless and a generation younger than the people in charge. Because they will have been encouraged instead of being restrained, they will develop into creative, assertive people who will work together with their individual talents to rebuild the earth.

Competition entry, 'My Ideal School'

History says, Don't hope
On this side of the grave
But then, once in a lifetime
The longed for tidal wave
Of justice can rise up,
And hope and history rhyme.

Seamus Heaney
The Cure at Troy

Nothing great was ever achieved without enthusiasm.

Ralph Waldo Emerson
Quoted in *The New Penguin Dictionary of Quotations*

The only place where success comes before work is in a dictionary.

Anon

Within the next two or three decades the global society will have to face up to, and make, a set of decisions the like of which humanity has never before faced …

I want these decisions made by people educated in the fullest sense of the word i.e. highly knowledgeable, capable of understanding complex problems, highly skilled, talented in the art of communication, confident working in teams, creative, and not least, capable of exercising moral judgement and taking a global perspective.

David Blunkett, MP
Raising Aspirations in the 21st Century

No education system can be world class without valuing and integrating creativity, in the curriculum, in management and leadership, and without linking this to promoting knowledge and understanding of cultural change and diversity.

K. Robinson
Out of Our Minds: Learning to be creative

The first step is to measure whatever can be easily measured. This is OK as far as it goes. The second step is to disregard that which can't be easily measured or to give it an arbitrary quantitative value. This is artificial and misleading. The third step is to presume that what can't be measured easily isn't really important. This is blindness. The fourth step is to say that what can't be easily measured really doesn't exist. This is suicide.

Robert Macnamara
Quoted in Charles B. Handy, *The Empty Raincoat*

I am enough of an artist to draw freely upon my imagination. Imagination is more important than knowledge. Knowledge is limited. Imagination encircles the world.

Albert Einstein
Out of My Later Years

Usually children spend more time in the garden than anybody else. It is where they learn about the world, because they can be in it unsupervised; yet protected. Some gardeners will remember from their own earliest recollections that no one sees the garden as vividly or cares about it as passionately, as the child who grows up in it.

Carol Williams
Bringing a Garden to Life

It often happens to children – and sometimes to gardeners – that they are given gifts the value of which they do not perceive until much later.

Wayne Winterrowd
Annuals for Connoisseurs

There is a garden in every childhood, an enchanted place where colours are brighter, the air softer, and the morning more fragrant than ever again.

Elizabeth Lawrence
Lob's Wood

Ever tried. Ever failed. No matter.
Try again. Fail again. Fail better.

Samuel Beckett
Wortsward Ho

You must learn to fail intelligently. Failing is one of the greatest arts in the world. One fails forward towards success.

Thomas Edison
Quoted in D.H. Hargreaves, *Working Laterally*

There is much to be said about failure. It is more interesting than success.

Max Beerbohm
Mainly on the Air

--->

I hear I forget
I see I remember
I do I learn
I reflect I improve

Kanwal I.S. Neel

◄---

A serious debate about failure is in fact a precondition of success. 'Success for all' and zero tolerance and failure turn out to be synonymous.

Michael Barber
The Learning Game: Arguments for an education revolution

The real voyage of discovery consists not in seeking new landscapes, but in having new eyes.

Marcel Proust

The best case for public education has always been that it is a common good. Everyone, ultimately, has a stake in the caliber of schools, and education is everyone's business.

Michael Fullan
The Moral Imperative of School Leadership

Education is not filling a pail but the lighting of a fire.

W.B. Yeats
Quoted in *Grey's Essential Miscellany for Teachers*

Success is a science; if you have the conditions, you get the result.

> Oscar Wilde
> Letter dated April 1883
> *The Oxford Dictionary of Humorous Quotations*

Success is relative: it is what we can make of the mess we have made of things.

> T.S. Eliot
> *A Family Reunion*

All you need in life is ignorance and confidence; then success is sure.

> Mark Twain
> Letter to Mrs Foote, 2 December 1887

It is not the mountain we conquer but ourselves.

> Edmund Hillary

As a human being, one has been endowed with just enough intelligence to be able to see clearly how utterly inadequate that intelligence is when confronted with what exists.

Albert Einstein
Quoted in *The Oxford Dictionary of Phrase, Saying, and Quotation*

Whoever in discussion adduces authority uses not intellect but rather memory.

Leonardo da Vinci
Notebooks

Things won are done; joy's soul lies in the doing.

William Shakespeare
Troilus and Cressida

The world is divided into people who do things
and people who get the credit. Try, if you can, to
belong to the first class. There's far less
competition.

Dwight Morrow
Letter to his son
Quoted in Harold Nicolson, *Dwight Morrow*

Education is when you read the fine print;
experience is what you get when you don't.

Pete Seeger
Quoted in Linda Botts, *Loose Talk*

Make sure you catch people doing something
well.

Charles B. Handy
Inside Organisations

Retain faith that you will prevail in the end, regardless of the difficulties and at the same time confront the brutal facts of your current reality, whatever they might be.

A.J. Stockdale
Quoted in M. Fullan, *The Moral Imperative of School Leadership*

What the best and wisest parent wants for his own child, that must the community want for all of its children. Any other ideal for our schools is narrow and unlovely; acted upon, it destroys our democracy.

John Dewey
Democracy and Education

Now what I want is, Facts. Teach these boys and girls nothing but Facts. Facts alone are wanted in life. Plant nothing else, and root out everything else … Stick to Facts, Sir!

Charles Dickens
Hard Times

If education is always to be conceived along the same and antiquated lines of a mere transition of knowledge, there is little to be hoped from it in the bettering of man's future. For what is the use of transmitting knowledge if the individual's total development lags behind?

Maria Montessori
The Absorbent Mind

I consider a human soul without education, like marble in the quarry, which shows none of its inherent beauties till the skill of the polisher fetches out the colours, makes the surface shine and discovers every ornamental daub spot and vein that runs through the body of it.

Joseph Addison
Quoted in *The International Education Quotations Encyclopaedia*

My ideal school could never exist. There is no reality in idealism. I dream of happiness and learning united. I dream of no interruptions. If I went to my ideal school I wouldn't wake up every morning and dread the next day, the next week, the next year, and the rest of my life. In my perfect school we would only have the teachers who knew and understood what they were talking about, they would all be passionate about their subjects and help us to unleash our passions. In my perfect school there would still be rules, but they would guide us, not confine us. Teachers and children would mesh harmoniously. There would be no grading, praise only for working hard not for your mental capability. I wouldn't have to try to compete with my friends and they wouldn't all want to (*sic*) better than each other. We would not be concerned about whether we did the best in the class, but only about whether everyone was happy with what he or she was doing and how he or she was progressing. There would still be punishment, but these punishments would matter to the student. They would have to miss their favourite lessons for a week and have to take double lessons of their worst subject instead.

We wouldn't be confined within walls of stone; we would go outside and experience the weather. We would travel and experience other pleasures. We would gain an understanding of the way of the world. Exams would be abolished, people would work together and alone, they would use other people's knowledge to enrich themselves and others would do the same with them. In my perfect school there would be no bullies, there would be no insecurities. We would discuss our opinions in every lesson and everyone would listen and respect each other. Teachers and pupils would be equals, no privileges or disadvantages; everyone would be in the same boat. In my school the only things they would ban would be unhappiness and pain, no room for lying, revenge and deceit.

But to have my perfect school you need a perfect world, and if the world were perfect there would be no room for dreaming.

Competition entry, 'My Ideal School'

What is an educational expert? The answer is simple. Practically everybody ... The only section of humanity to whom the title is denied are the people who have to teach.

Ian Hay

To me education is leading out of what is already there in the pupil's soul. To Miss Mackay it is putting in of something that is not there, and that is not what I call education, I call it intrusion.

Muriel Spark
The Prime of Miss Jean Brodie

If thou of fortune be bereft
And of thine earthly store have left
Two loaves, sell one and with the dole
Buy hyacinths to feed the soul.

Moslih Eddin Saadi
Garden of Roses

The principal goal of education in schools should be creating men and women who are capable of doing things, not only repeating what other generations have done.

Jean Piaget
The Origins of Intelligence in Children

Human history becomes more and more a race between education and catastrophe.

H.G. Wells
The Outline of History

Chapter 2

Leadership and management

> The Leader is best
> When people barely know that he exists,
> Not so good when people obey and acclaim him,
> Worst when they despise him.
> Fail to honour people,
> They will fail to honour you.
> But of a good leader, who talks little,
> When his work is done, his aim fulfilled,
> They will say, 'We did it ourselves'.
>
> Lao Tzu
> *Tao Te Ching* (600Bc)

One of the quotations we have used in this book is to the effect that most UK organizations are underled and overmanaged. But there is only one thing worse: organizations that are overled and undermanaged. We need both.

We've been living in a period when the prevailing wisdom has emphasized the overwhelming importance of leadership. Both of us can remember the time when the reverse was the case. In the 1970s Henley was set up as a Management College for managers in industry, business and commerce. In 2001 however the National College for School Leadership – not management – was created.

We came across a collection of points and counterpoints describing transformational and transactional leaders which, in its value-laden way, is set out opposite. There are many points in the right-hand, 'Transactional', column that are desirable within any organization. But there are some that are not. It is not simply doing the right thing, it's often necessary for the smooth running of an organization like a school to do things right. Despite the validity of some of the statements in the right-hand column of the table we suspect they were put together by someone keener on leadership than management of the necessarily transactional type.

Management

When we look at the schools which appear to have got things right in terms of both their smooth running and high staff morale they have some of the following management features.

Staff handbook

The staff handbook is in loose-leaf as well as electronic form and is ritualistically altered as needed at staff briefings. Its features include essentially a description of policy on any issue, the implications for practices and who is responsible for leading changes and who else for the tasks needed. All on no more than two sides of A4.

People always talk about 'consistency' – or use the phrase 'singing from the same song sheet'. But of course striking the right balance between what can be left to individual discretion and 'what we all do' is the elusive question, the correct answer

LEADERSHIP	
TRANSFORMATIONAL	**TRANSACTIONAL**
Builds on the need for meaning	Builds on need to get the job done and make a living
Preoccupied with purposes, values, morals and ethics	Preoccupied with power and position, politics and perks
Transcends daily affairs	Swamped in daily affairs
Oriented towards long-term goals without compromising human values and principles	Oriented to short-term goals and hard data
Separates causes and symptoms and works at prevention	Confuses causes and symptoms and is concerned with treatment
Aligns internal structures and systems to reinforce overarching values and goals	Supports structures and systems that reinforce the bottom line
Focuses more on missions and strategies for achieving them	Focuses on tactical issues
Makes full use of available resources (human)	Relies on human relationship to oil human interactions
Designs and redesigns jobs to make them meaningful and challenging; realizes human potential	Follows and fulfils role expectations by striving to work effectively within current systems

to which will vary from school to school at different times and in different circumstances. Get it wrong in one direction and chaos beckons; err in the other and people feel oppressed and powerless. Nevertheless the 'staff handbook' should be the living document that all the school staff – primary phase and subject co-ordinators, secondary faculties, Key Stage and Year heads of secondary – observe. And they will observe it because each policy and set of practices described there will be testament to the shared values of the leaders and the whole school community. The 'worry factor' leadership responsibility for any particular policy and its implementation will be on the A4 sheet. Moreover, everyone will know how and when to make a contribution to the collective review of any policy and practice. So if they are keen on change they can't say they haven't had a chance to have their say.

Job descriptions

Job descriptions will have 'lead' and 'support' responsibilities. Most job descriptions have always been a long list of duties and tasks rounded off by 'such other duties as shall from time to time be determined'. They are enough to make the most long-suffering and patient saint feel put upon!

Far better are job descriptions which talk about 'lead' or 'primary' responsibility in areas where the person is responsible and 'support' responsibility for other things where the job holder acts as a team member. More than most organizations schools need this sort of job description, since they are usually a complex matrix or web of teams. For example in a secondary school a single individual may be second in charge of geography with lead responsibility for curriculum in Key Stage 3, a history teacher in Key Stage 3, a geography A level teacher and a tutor in Year 8. So they belong to the Year 8 team, keep themselves supportively abreast of history, have a lead and support responsibility in geography and are part of the sixth form team. Schools are complex places where people get exhausted, while the rest of us get tired. Their job descriptions are written and revised in conjunction with the staff handbook. How they are framed makes a huge difference.

The CAT analysis: self-evaluation made easy

Behind each policy is a set of practices. From time to time they are reviewed. The leader for each activity is in the staff handbook, which states when reviews will take place. Review is best done invitationally and openly. So those keen to contribute can, since the more who can be involved the better. They collect evidence – data from exams, tests and surveys, case studies, observations, reports of external reviewers. They use the evidence they've collected to begin the process of evaluating what's gone well and not so well, and then speculate about change. That's where the CAT comes in. Mostly – unless the school or section has become dysfunctional – people will want to (C) confirm what existing practices and policies are. But there will be a lot of (A) adjusting or tinkering to fine-tune practices to be better fit for purpose. Finally – and only rarely – the school will need to (T) transform its practices.

Outstanding schools, like outstanding teachers, never think they have arrived. They are always anxious to model the example of what they ceaselessly encourage all their students to adopt in their behaviour and expectations – namely, 'improve on previous best'. So there's a lot of 'adjusting' to do.

The use of data: the management information system and the e-learning platform

This has to be regarded as work in progress. But it's promising work. We've visited schools which have achieved some sort of transformation of what's possible through the extraordinarily well-developed use of ICT and its systems. So many schools have equipped their staff with laptops and have created their own intranet of learning materials and put them on an e-learning platform – like Kaleidos for example – which then blends (on an accessible and personalized portal) their computer-centred learning materials for use with important management information – absence, punctuality, behaviour incidents, students' school reports and data on pupil performance. The system also holds an exhaustive list of homework tasks, so that homework is not left to chance but can be referred to by teacher and student alike. The same applies to lesson plans. For the system is then accessible – with safeguards – variously to teachers, support staff, students and parents.

To some who read this, such a system may seem daunting, to others it is already a reality. Every medium to large school, whether primary or secondary – though it's not, of course, appropriate for a two- or three-teacher primary school – should aim to have such a system in place by 2007/8 at the latest. It will transform the energy of students and staff alike. But – our point already made – it will take more than vision about this ICT-driven scheme: it will take meticulous, persistent and skilled management effort.

There are countless other practices where schools need to get the detail right – parent consultations, lunchtimes, awards ceremonies, assemblies, timetables, the collection of monies, induction, cover, the keeping of accounts. It is not the purpose of this brief document to illustrate ways of improving each. But all can be improved. All require detailed management.

The school calendar and timetable

Schools are aware of the irritation and frustration that can occur when people arrange events which clash. That's why the school calendar and how and when it's possible to get events linked is a key factor. The school timetable is also important and especially the power of the timetabler, whose decisions about who teaches whom and where so vitally affect the likelihood of learning taking place successfully.

Leadership

But the other side of the same coin is leadership. In all the thousands of books, all the studies, all the courses are there a few essentials which we can distil into a few hundred words? We think there are.

There are three points to be made about leadership. Firstly, it requires skills as well as abilities; secondly, it comes in different (and we think equally effective) styles, with a value and behaviour system common to each; thirdly, it involves tasks.

Whether one's leading in a classroom, in a faculty or the whole school it's essential to have 'energy, enthusiasm and hope'. We use 'hope', not 'optimism' – because there is the promise of delivery: it's a matter of determination, not opinion. When someone said that teachers and headteachers needed 'unwarranted optimism', that's what they were getting at. Leaders will regard crisis as the norm and complexity as fun. They will experience a lot of both. They need an endless well of intellectual curiosity to feed speculation about what's possible, to keep asking questions rather than continually provide the answers. This is stimulated by their listening, reading and writing habits: neglect any and you are putting your leadership standards at risk. Finally, they need a complete absence of paranoia and self-pity. As a leader, whether of maths or the whole school, you are credited with seeing further and wider on that topic than others. You make coherence. To make coherence of the leaders of maths or English and so on the head needs to listen and put their expert knowledge about maths or English together in a coherent whole, while simultaneously making sense of the context – the local community, the national changes, the turnover of staff and students, the availability of resources. Vitally, they fit this into a view of the future that translates into a collective vision for the school community.

Inevitably – however much the process is shared, as it should be – the leader in a large organization cannot be in continuous touch with the various stakeholders. They will make regular systematic contact – replete with acts of unexpected kindness and thoughtfulness – but the contact cannot be constant. It is essentially important that at times of crisis the leader digs deep into determination and doesn't fall prey to self-pity.

The two enabling skills of leadership are delegation and time.

Delegation

Nine levels of delegation

1   Look into this problem. Give me all the facts. I will decide what to do.

2   Let me know the options available, with the pros and cons of each. I will decide what to select.

3   Let me know the criteria for your recommendation, which alternatives you have identified and which one appears best to you, with any risk identified. I will make the decision.

4   Recommend a course of action for my approval.

5   Let me know what you intend to do. Delay action until I approve.

6   Let me know what you intend to do. Do it unless I say not to.

7   Take action. Let me know what you did. Let me know how it turns out.

8   Take action. Communicate with me only if action is unsuccessful.

9   Take action. No further communication with me is necessary.

The list above sets out the possible positions when determining how and when to delegate. Clearly, as we relax or revert to type, we will all have our preferred position, but will have learned the skill of deliberately deciding where to be on the spectrum of possible positions with different people for different tasks. So you may feel that someone new in a job will require some support as they adjust to new surroundings but decide later that they are at, for example, number 7, 8 or 9 for most things. Indeed you'd be bothered if you needed to be at 2, 3 or 4 – and desperate if you needed to be at 1!

Being aware of this spectrum is therefore a helpful guide to the need for extended professional development for others – or oneself.

One final word of caution about delegation. The surest way of consuming energy and demotivating or disempowering staff is to tell them they are at number 7 in the box but at the height of a crisis or in external matters regret it too late and tell them subsequently they were at number 5!

Time

Leaders – as the Shaw quotation shows – can be so driven and committed that it isn't simply that they live to work but they become totally consumed by the work, almost workaholics. What drives most people in large organizations into this trap is that they find it difficult to say 'no' to the legitimate requests for time from certain stakeholders. So, as headteacher, of course you need to attend performances, sports events, contributions and give time to the local community. (Perhaps that's why, as things accumulate over time – research says seven years – leaders need to seek new pastures!)

Yet in the end, while taking responsibility for things that go wrong is part and parcel of every leader's responsibility, so too is encouraging others to take risks and then backing their judgement. This takes time and nerve. Ask questions rather than provide answers. Having a notice on the back of your office door, 'Leave this to me', with a big line through it is an ever-present reminder that you don't want to suck decisions towards you when people visit. For that matter, why have an office to yourself anyway, when you could share with a senior colleague(s) so that ideas are shared and grow in the process? Better also to meet colleagues on their own ground rather than always get them to come to you.

In short, there are a number of activities that will fill a leader's time. We reckon there are six:

Firstly, they create energy

Their own example – what they say, what they believe, who they are – is one of indomitable will and a passion for success that is at once courageous and brooks no denial. They talk not about staff but with staff. They ask 'what if' speculative questions. They are fussy about appointments, taking care not to make permanent appointments of 'energy consumers'. Because they are full of hope they look for optimists – those who say 'how we could' rather than 'why we can't'. They show interest in every aspect of school life.

Secondly, they build capacity

Again, they set an example. They teach themselves and are observed by staff doing so, or they take over a class to let others observe somebody else's practice. They rotate the chairing of meetings to grow the skill of others. They ensure young staff members are involved in a 'school improvement group' and act on their suggestions. They have a programme for staff development that considers the better future of individuals as well as of the school. They know and cherish all the interests of all staff – especially those which the staff used to do in previous jobs or do in the world beyond school. They use the collective first person pronoun 'we' rather than the singular 'I'. They take the blame when it's not their fault and they are generous with praise to others for collective success. They set an example of learning, for instance by adopting an annual learning plan. They read and share articles and encourage others to do the same.

Thirdly, they meet and minimize crisis

At a time of genuine crisis they find cause for optimism and hope, for points of learning. They stay calm. They acknowledge their own mistakes. They are 'pogo-stick' players in the sense that they can simultaneously be in the thick of things, as it were, yet still be seeing the wider picture. A present crisis is the source for vital learning and future improvement. They themselves show willing to be a 'utility player' – one who, *in extremis*, will turn their hand to any task.

Fourthly, they secure and enhance the environment

They ensure classroom teaching and learning materials are well organized and in plentiful supply. They make sure the management arrangements are seen by staff as 'fit for purpose' – right in detail and serving the needs of both staff and students alike.

For example, they often review meetings to ensure that 'transactional' or 'business' meetings are minimized. The staff handbook is repeatedly updated and the computer system works and provides a useful database for staff, all of whom have laptops, and for students, who, with parents, have access at school and remotely to lesson plans, to homework tasks, to reports and to progress grades. They improve the staffroom and the whole environment of school – both visually and aurally.

Fifthly, they seek and chart improvement

They themselves use comparative benchmarking data both within school and from other schools. They are keen on 'benchmarking', but they do so in a climate of encouraging risk.

They themselves ensure there is a proper mix of 'appreciative enquiry' and problem solving. Appreciative enquiry involves finding and celebrating what's good and engaging in a search for what's outstanding – by visiting other practitioners and finding out what research tells us – before deciding on a plan of action to deliver excellence. This is a process of 'energy creation'! Problem solving, on the other hand, concerns staff with barriers and problems that have cropped up. They require analysis and the creation of possible solutions before deciding on a plan of action. This is a frequently necessary process – but it consumes energy, more in some people than in others. So the successful leader, conscious of this, seeks to create a climate of much appreciative enquiry to handle the inevitable energy consumption when solving problems.

Those who seek and chart improvement celebrate genuine – it must be genuine – success. And they know the best of 'genuine' is an improvement on past practice, whether individual or collective. But they celebrate other social events too – to create the climate in which energy, capacity and ultimate success depend. So governors' meetings and staff meetings, awards ceremonies and 'briefings' are crucial to that.

They are, above all, good at 'collective' as opposed to 'individual' monitoring.

Sixthly and lastly, they are always extending the vision of what's possible

Clearly, this involves being both historian and futurologist. Any leader wishing to extend the vision of what's possible is deeply aware of this double requirement, especially since the present dominates so much of school life. And if sometimes that present seems overwhelming, the energy levels drop. So telling stories which remind people of past success and which honour successful predecessors and the school's history is a thing wise leaders do. But they are also forecasters of the weather and describers of future possibilities. They confidently describe a path from the present to the future. They are good listeners and readers. They write 'future' pieces for their community. They ask 'why not' aloud and 'why' silently in their heads.

Quotations

This is the true joy in life, being used for a purpose recognised by yourself as a mighty one … being part of a great enterprise rather than a feverish selfish little clod of ailments complaining that the world won't devote itself to making you happy. I want to be thoroughly used up when I die, for the more I work, the more I live. Life is no brief candle to me. It's a sort of splendid torch which I've got hold of for the moment. And I want to make it burn as brightly as possible before handing it on to future generations.

George Bernard Shaw
Man and Superman

Leadership and learnership are indispensable to one another.

Attributed to John F. Kennedy

The great gift of leadership is to bring about the gifts of followship in everybody else.

Michael Fullan
The Moral Imperative of School Leadership

Leaders cannot be taught – but leaders can be educated.

Anon

There is a difference between leadership and management. Leadership is of the spirit, compounded of personality and vision; its practice is an art. Management is of the mind, a matter of accurate calculation … its practice is a science. Managers are necessary; leaders are essential.

Field Marshal Lord Slim
Quoted in Van Maurik, *Writers on Leadership*

He fed into their spirits by many means: by humour, dedicated example and that romanticism that talked defeats away as if they were fleeting embarrassments that a malevolent and dishonest fate had inflicted ... they worked so well that his players never allowed defeat to become a habit.

Hugh McIlveny
The Observer, obituary for Bill Shankly

In successful school leadership density rules.

T.J. Sergiovanni
Leadership: What's in it for schools?

The first rule of leadership is that it is shared.

Tim Brighouse and David Woods
How to Improve Your School

- Transactional Leaders (Managers)
  - Main job is planning, budgeting, organising, staffing, controlling, problem solving and producing degrees of predictability and order.
- Transformational Leaders (Leaders)
  - Main job is to establish direction, align people, motivate and inspire, and to produce and sustain change.
  - Being who they are, they 'transform their followers'.
- Managers derive their role from their position; Leaders must earn and win influence from those around them.

Leader–Managers

- Most UK organisations are over managed and under led.
- Strong leadership with weak management is no better.
- The real challenge is to combine strong leadership and strong management.
- Leader–Managers are what organisations need.
- Institutionalising a Leader–Manager centred culture is the ultimate act of leadership.

J.P. Kotter
'What Leaders Really Do'

Six Leadership Styles

1 Coercive – the leader demands compliance.
   ('Do what I tell you.')

2 Authoritative – the leader motivates people
   towards the vision.

3 Affiliative – the leader creates harmony and
   builds emotional bonds.
   ('People come first.')

4 Democratic – the leader forges consensus
   through participation.
   ('What do you think?')

5 Pacesetting – the leader sets high standards
   for performance.
   ('Do as I do, now.')

6 Coaching – the leader develops people for
   the future.
   ('Try this.')

Hay McBer
Research into Teacher Effectiveness

We cannot become what we need to be by
remaining as we are.

Anon

In a learning organisation, leaders are DESIGNERS, STEWARDS and TEACHERS. They are responsible for building organisations where people continually expand their capabilities to understand complexity, clarify vision and improve shared mental models – that is, they are responsible for learning.

- Designers – The leader's task is designing the learning process whereby people throughout the organisation can deal productively with the issues they face.

- Stewards – Leaders continually seek and oversee the broader purposes and direction of the organisation by sharing and developing the vision.

- Teachers – Leaders in the learning organisation foster learning for everyone and help people develop systematic understandings.

Michael Fullan
Change Forces (1993)

Leadership for transformation is the art of accomplishing more than the science of management says is possible.

Attributed to Colin Powell

One of the key principles of leadership is that leaders must strive to be model learners. They must continue to read, and engage in discussions about all manner of subjects as well as the most recent theories of learning. As leaders they should question current practices, and never feel that they have progressed beyond the point of being a learner. Learning is truly a lifelong experience, and cannot be thought of simply as a destination.

T.J. Sergiovanni
Leadership: What's in it for schools?

Teachers who choose teacher leadership become owners and investors in their schools, rather than mere tenants.

Roland S. Barth
Improving Schools from Within

Leaders are ... persons who, by word and/or personal example, markedly influence the behaviours, thoughts and/or feelings of a significant number of their fellow human beings.

Howard Gardner
Leading Minds: Anatomy of leadership

Good leaders are adept at reframing problems, at putting old facts into new bottles, or reconceptualizing the familiar so that new solutions leap up.

Charles B. Handy
Inside Organisations

Good leaders are almost always great simplifiers who can cut through argument, debate and doubt, to offer a solution that everybody can understand.

Attributed to Colin Powell

Outstanding leaders have a vision for their schools – a mental picture of a preferred future – which is shared with all in the school community and which shapes the programme for learning and teaching as well as policies, priorities, plans and procedures pervading the day-to-day life of the school.

Beare, Caldwell and Millikan
Creating an Excellent School

Leadership is action, not position.

Anon

Perpetual optimism is a force multiplier. The ripple effect of a leader's enthusiasm is awesome. So is the impact of cynicism and pessimism. Spare me the grim litany of the 'realist', give me the unrealistic aspirations of the optimist any day.

Attributed to Colin Powell

Leadership, like jazz, is a public performance, dependent on so many things – the environment, the volunteers in the band, the need for everybody to perform as individuals and as a group, the absolute dependence of the leader on the members of the band.

Max De Pree
Leadership Jazz

Leaders set the course for the organisation; managers make sure the course is followed. Leaders make strategic plans; managers design operational systems for carrying out the plans. Leaders stimulate and inspire; managers use their interpersonal influence and authority to translate that energy into productive work.

K.S. Louis and M.B. Miles
Improving the Urban High School

Leadership is to the current decade what standards were to the 1990s for those interested in large-scale reform. Standards, even when well implemented, can take us only part way to large-scale reform. It is only leadership that can take us all the way.

Michael Fullan
Change Forces with a Vengeance

School leadership is a profoundly moral, ethical and emotional activity designed to encourage a school's staff to build and act on a shared and evolving vision of enhanced educational experiences for pupils.

Stoll, Fink and Earl
It's About Learning and it's About Time

Level 5 leaders blend extreme personal humility with intense professional will.

Jim Collins
Good to Great

Level Five Leaders

- Are ambitious for their organisation, not for themselves
- Talk about their organisation, not about themselves
- Have a dogged, unwavering, ferocious resolve
- Are fanatically driven with an incurable need to produce substantial results
- Are more like plough horses than show horses
- Apportion credit to events outside themselves when things go well
- Take personal responsibility when things go badly
- Set up their successors for even greater success.

Jim Collins
Good to Great

Courage is rightly esteemed the first of human qualities because as has been said, it is the quality which guarantees all others.

Winston S. Churchill
Great Contemporaries

--➤

I keep six honest serving men,
(they taught me all I know),
Their names are what and why and when
and how and where and who.

Rudyard Kipling
Just So Stories

◄---

A good leader is also a good follower.

American proverb

We trained hard ... but it seemed that every time
we were beginning to form up into teams we
would be reorganised. I was to learn later in life
that we tend to meet any new situation by
reorganising; and a wonderful method it can be
for creating the illusion of progress while
producing confusion, inefficiency, and
demoralisation.

Late twentieth-century saying
Cited in *The Oxford Dictionary of Phrase, Saying, and Quotation*

Start with good people, lay out the rules, communicate with your employees, motivate them and reward them. If you do all these things effectively, you can't miss.

Lee Iacocca
Talking Straight

The task of leadership is not to put greatness into humanity but to elicit it, for the greatness is already there.

John Buchan
Montrose and Leadership

Butterflies

How headteachers know all their students

Description

The headteacher and senior deputy personally introduce Year 7 students in their first term to the school's history and traditions through illustrated presentations. Every student is taught ICT by the senior deputy. In May the headteacher leads Year 7 on their residential camp. In June the headteacher and deputy lead Year 7 and their tutors in African Dance Week.

To promote this smooth transfer the illustrated presentations consist of an ongoing photographic record of the school's history and achievements. We make a photographic record of each year's main events, for example, junior and senior concerts; drama and the school show; outdoor education, with Key Stage 3 tutor group visits to Derbyshire, the headteacher's Year 7 Lake District Camp, the Year 9 Dover Camp and Summer School, sports tours and curriculum competitions. Each year, the most powerful images of these activities are selected and printed on canvas in the form of banners which are displayed in the main corridors of the school. After each activity a selection of images is played for the next few days on the video screen in the school foyer.

Comment on impact

In all schools the senior students are generally known by the headteacher and deputy and the senior students know them. However, in this school this is achieved by the end of Year 7. This also means that the headteacher and deputy know the whole school of 1,507 students.

Students and staff are proud of their school, their friends and their colleagues. Year 7 students are proud to raise the school flag each day.

Students, staff and visitors like the large-scale images. They create a positive achievement culture where students are pleased to see their family and friends taking part in the school's activities.

Staff remain committed to school trips and journeys despite a climate of legal threat and negativity. Last year 80 per cent of the staff were involved in a school visit of one kind or another.

Year groups and individuals are regularly reminded of the legend they are creating.

Work shadowing key posts in the school

Description

Ensuring that other colleagues develop some expertise in particular key areas in addition to that of the member of staff who has a designated responsibility for that area; for example, cover, timetabling, school budgeting, examination procedures and administration. Areas in which this was already taking place would include work experience and certain pastoral positions.

Comment on impact

In addition to ensuring a smooth transition in the event of collision with the proverbial bus, this would give colleagues an additional experience to contribute to their career development. This would allow the sharing of ideas and the benefit that always comes from having another point of view, thus developing a team approach. In time the 'shadow' may well take overall responsibility for that area and allow colleagues to move on to another area to develop a new expertise. In this way staff avoid becoming entrenched in one area, and new opportunities can be opened up as the cycle moves on.

This has implications for the way 'job descriptions' are written. They are often long lists of tasks with the 'stomach sinking' final one of 'such other duties as may ...'. What this butterfly implants is a job description where there are 'leading' or 'primary' responsibilities with 'secondary' or 'support' responsibilities.

Distributed leadership

Description

To spread leadership and avoid an 'us' and 'them' culture, the senior leadership team appointed both a middle leader and a young member of staff to their team, each for a term. Expectations did not involve extra responsibility, but just attending meetings and respecting confidentiality. Although the first participants needed prompting to volunteer, there was soon a steady stream of would-be participants.

Comment on impact

The school considered the 'us' and 'them' culture had been largely turned round, commenting that at least the 'challenges' they sometimes legitimately face from staff are better informed and come with a heightened respect for the long hours and hard work any senior leadership team has to accept. Staff get a better insight into whole school issues and strategic management.

Chapter 3

Teaching

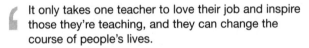

> It only takes one teacher to love their job and inspire
> those they're teaching, and they can change the
> course of people's lives.
>
> 'Skin' (Deborah Dyer)
> Interview, *Times Educational Supplement* (2006)

We were both part of a Birmingham delegation to Chicago in the mid-1990s – an educational summit between the two cities, each described by their respective national education secretaries as 'the worst education authority in our country'.

Chicago's chief executive Paul Vallas reckoned that out of his 22,000 teachers only 2,000 were good. We said we were well placed because out of 10,000 Birmingham teachers 9,900 were either good or outstanding. Chicago pined for a 'teaching bible' covering every eventuality, to which the teacher could turn for guidance in any circumstance. We shrugged our shoulders and looked doubtful. Ten years on Chicago is still struggling to shake off its label of the 'worst in the country' while Birmingham is regarded as an example of how city schools can transform themselves. We believe therefore that how you treat teachers is a powerful influence on how well they perform and who is attracted to teaching.

Why start with this story? Well, for two reasons. First, stories are, of course, the stock-in-trade of good teachers, if – and it's an important if – the stories have a purpose. That highlights the second reason, for our story carries a message. Both the Chicago chief executive and we were wrong. We overestimated the number of good and successful teachers while he grossly underestimated it. He was 'ensuring compliance' and 'problem solving' with his projected 'teaching ten commandments' while we were practising 'appreciative enquiry'. The use of those three phrases – 'problem solving', 'appreciative enquiry' and 'ensuring compliance' – owes everything to business psychological theory. Three columns in the table below set out four stages for each activity. According to the theorists, 'appreciative enquiry' builds energy while 'problem solving' – a necessary part of all aspects of life – consumes it.

	Appreciative Enquiry	**Problem Solving**	**Ensuring Compliance**
1	Appreciate the best of 'what is'	Find a felt need; identify the problem	Decide what is right
2	Envision 'what might be'	Analyse causes	Promulgate single solutions
3	Dialogue for new knowledge and theory 'what should be'	Analyse solutions	Regulate and inspect
4	Create the vision 'what will be'	Develop an action plan	Punish in public deviants and inadequates

One of the features of successful teachers – who are 'energy creators' who see the glass as 'half full', a 'silver lining in every cloud' and ask 'What if?!' – is that they use three or four parts of appreciative enquiry for every one problem they need to solve. Meanwhile unsuccessful teachers – who are energy consumers who see the glass as 'half empty', 'clouds for every silver lining' and say 'What more can you expect from these children?' – become enforcers of compliance at the expense of appreciative enquiry as they wrestle with their mounting problems.

The children in the classrooms of energy creators and appreciative enquirers have a much more successful experience than those in the classrooms of energy consumers and enforcers of compliance.

So our first two points about teaching are that the disposition and attitude of teachers are crucial and that important though well-rehearsed classroom management and organizational skills are – including the three-, four- or five-part lesson with plenaries – they are not enough. We set out below the characteristics and qualities of good teachers.

Good Teachers
Qualities and Characteristics

Good understanding of self and of interpersonal relationships

Generosity of spirit

Sense of humour

Sharp observational powers

Interest in and concern for others

Infectious enthusiasm for what is taught

Imagination

Intellectual curiosity

Professional training and understanding of how children learn

Ability to plan programmes of learning appropriate to the particular groups of children and individual students

Understanding of their curriculum in the context of the school as a whole

So if disposition and attitude are important, what more can we say about them in the outstanding teacher? Outstanding teachers genuinely believe that all children can learn successfully and that they can teach anyone to succeed. They have learning goals for themselves, both for the subject and the way they teach. They try out new ideas. Their teaching is therefore a competence to be continuously increased and they grow learning competence in their students. They practise 'assessment for learning', whereby the learner becomes aware of the next stage of learning and knows how to extend the learning already made. These teachers do not so much differentiate the groups they teach, rather they differentiate themselves. They believe that effort on the student's part in learning is not a sign of limited ability. They make learning fun and exude hope, energy and enthusiasm. They behave as if learning is a co-operative authority – 'we can crack this algebraic problem together, Class 9, can't we?' – and harness learning as a group as well as an individual activity, thereby importing to the classroom (with all the positive messages of collaboration) the gang nature of the playground or the street – where its consequences are often negative and disastrous. Above all, they believe in the 'transformability' of their youngsters as opposed to their 'ability'.

Teachers work on the cusp of the axis between 'self-esteem' and 'expectation'. If expectation is too high and the students' self-esteem too low, the students will fail to learn and the teacher fail to teach. The other way round – students' self-esteem ahead of teacher's expectations – is almost as serious. We say 'almost', because in these circumstances older students with higher order learning competence will learn despite the teacher. The issue is to pitch expectation, both for the group and for the individual, just a bit ahead of where the students have reached.

So all teachers work at self-esteem. They greet children positively in the morning, speak to children by name, not just in the classroom but in the corridor and at lunchtimes. They create a shared past and teach good stories about their students, who know they are expected to contribute to the 'legacy' of the school. They share in the interests of the young, whether it be pop stars, soaps, sport or food. They remember birthdays, recognize the achievements of youngsters elsewhere, whether in the school or beyond the school. They mark privately and confess to a private interest. When a student baffles them and when they can't, as it were, make contact – they seek out an article or artefact at the weekend which they know resonates with the student's interest. Then they quietly give it to the youngster with the words: 'I saw this and thought of you'. In short, they are masters of the unexpected. In their students' eyes they appear safely and interestingly unpredictable.

In the field of expectation they use story, are expert in questioning techniques and involve their students in leadership.

Good teachers ensure that their students are at least as busy as they are! Students – after applying for various jobs as classroom managers – know it's their job to monitor attendance, to mind the computer, to organize resources, to collect in books at the ends of lessons, or whatever. Teachers in such classrooms deploy a marking practice that makes students feel special. They provide extensive private written feedback to each student at least twice a year. They are such masters of 'assessment for learning' that students become able to assess their own and other people's work. In doing so, their students become more and more active and competent autonomous learners.

These teachers understand and use different techniques appealing to the visual, the auditory and the kinesthetic.

This is the bread and butter of all good teachers. Our quotations and butterflies, however, are designed to inspire the quest of the teacher in moving from good to outstanding.

Quotations

For HMI the answers or advice seldom lie in one or the other; in either or, but usually in both, in a balance along a spectrum such as: whole class teaching together with small group work, subject focused and child centred, imaginative flights and sound grammatical syntax, discrete and disseminated teaching, explicit and implicit teaching of skills, out of context and in context, inductive and deductive approaches, facts and fancy, talk and silence, being shown and finding out for oneself, computers and pencils, manual craft and electronic skills, books and CD ROM, handwritten letters and e-mail, education for self and for the economy ... so, the matter is literacy and language.

Simon Clements, HMI
Presentation to Rotherham Schools (1994)

There is no higher calling. Without teachers, society would slide back into primitive squalor.

Ted Wragg: A Tribute, TES/Routledge (2006)

Teachers, like artisans, work mainly alone, cobbling together ideas and materials out of which, through repeated tinkering, they devise strategies and routines to make teaching and learning work effectively in variable conditions.

Michael Huberman
'Teacher Development and Instruction of Mastery'

You can't just walk into an urban high school and lecture; you'd lose the students. You have to dance with them; be a drill sergeant, priest, minister, shoulder to cry on and housekeeper. Like Toscanini and a master psychologist rolled into one.

Frank McCourt
Interview, *Times Educational Supplement* (2005)

It is the supreme art of the teacher to awaken joy in creative expression and knowledge.

Albert Einstein
Out of My Later Years

I was supposed to be a welfare statistic … It is because of a teacher that I sit at this table. I remember her telling us one cold, miserable day that she could not make our clothing better; she could not provide us with food; she could not change the terrible segregated conditions under which we lived. She could introduce us to the world of reading, the world of books and that is what she did.

What a world! I visited Asia and Africa. I saw magnificent sunsets; I tasted exotic foods; I fell in love and danced in wonderful halls. I ran away with escaped slaves and stood beside a teenage martyr. I visited lakes and streams and composed lines of verse. I knew then that I wanted to help children do the same things, I wanted to weave magic.

From evidence submitted to the
National Commission on Teaching and America's Future (1999)

I teach because I search.

Paolo Freire
Pedagogy of the Oppressed

It is a pity that the notion of 'creativity' in education has to be fought for or reclaimed, as it should be a central feature of teaching and learning. It is the crucial element in each generation's renewal and enhancement of itself. Without it society would roll backwards. Human imaginations and spirit are what drive civilisation forward.

E.C. Wragg
The Art and Science of Teaching and Learning

As a teacher you're not only a writer but an actor, a parent, a director and an improviser – it's not so much a Hollywood epic as a low budget movie with a hand-held camera.

Jonathan Smith
The Learning Game

Whatever you are teaching make it clear. Make it as firm as a stone and as bright as sunlight.

Gilbert Highet
The Art of Teaching

Classrooms are crowded and busy places in which groups of students who vary in interests and abilities must be directed. Moreover these groups assemble regularly for long periods of time to accomplish a wide variety of tasks. Many events occur simultaneously, the teachers must react often and immediately to circumstances, and the course of events is frequently unpredictable. Teaching in such settings requires a highly developed ability to manage events.

W. Doyle
'Classroom Knowledge as a Foundation for Teaching'

Teaching should be a profession in which creative and adventurous, but hard headed pioneers feel at home.

D.H. Hargreaves
Creative Professionalism

Imagine that you would become a better teacher just by virtue of being on the staff of a particular school – just from that fact alone.

Judith W. Little
The Power of Organisational Setting

Teachers affect eternity, they can never tell where their influence stops.

Henry Brook Adams
The Education of Henry Adams

Good colleagues inspire and encourage each other ... good colleagues compliment and complement each other ... They keep themselves and they keep each other alive.

Jonathan Smith
The Learning Game

Teaching should be acknowledged as a top profession. Some go even further and put it above all others, because teachers have the ability to unlock the potential of the rest of society.

Estelle Morris
Professionalism and Trust

Everyone is a staff developer for everyone else.

Anon

One of the greatest challenges of teaching is to describe what you want to be as a teacher, what you care about and how you will conduct yourself with students.

William Ayers
To Teach

Desire is at the heart of good teaching … the desire for fulfilment, influence, achievement, sense of breakthrough, closeness to fellow humans … in desire is to be found the creativity and spontaneity that connects teachers emotionally and sensually (in the literal sense of feeling) to their children, their colleagues and their work …

A. Hargreaves
Changing Teachers, Changing Times

The mediocre teacher tells
The good teacher explains
The superior teacher demonstrates
The great teacher inspires.

William Arthur Ward
Quoted in *Grey's Essential Miscellany for Teachers*

Scratch a good teacher and you find a moral purpose.

Michael Fullan
Change Forces with a Vengeance

We know we are in a good school when the four following things obtain:

- Teachers talk about teaching and learning;
- Teachers observe each other's practice;
- Teachers plan, organise, deliver, monitor and evaluate their work together;
- Teachers teach others.

Judith W. Little
The Power of Organisational Setting

Those of us who work in the field of education are neither bank clerks who have little discretion nor assembly line workers whose actions are largely repetitive. Each child we teach is wonderfully unique and each requires us to use in our work that most exquisite of human capacities, the ability to make judgements in the absence of rules. Although good teaching uses routines, it is seldom routine. Good teaching depends on sensibility and imagination. It courts surprise. It profits from caring. In short, good teaching is an artistic affair.

Elliot W. Eisner
The Educational Imagination

Of some of our teachers, we remember their foibles and mannerisms, of others, their kindness and encouragement, or their fierce devotion to standards of work that we probably did not share at the time. And of those who inspired us most, we remember what they cared about, and that they cared about us, and the person we might become. It is the quality of caring about ideas and values, this fascination with the potential for growth within people, this depth and fervour about doing things well and striving for excellence, that comes closest to what I mean in describing a 'passionate teacher'.

Robert L. Fried
The Passionate Teacher

Teaching is an act of hope for a better future ... the reward of teaching is knowing that your life makes a difference.

William Ayers
To Teach

Educational change depends on what teachers do and think.

Michael Fullan
The New Meaning of Educational Change

To be a passionate teacher is to be someone in love with a field of knowledge, deeply stirred by issues and ideas that challenge our world, drawn to the dilemmas and potential of the young people who come into class each day, captivated by all of these. A passionate teacher is a teacher who breaks out of the isolation of a classroom, who refuses to submit to apathy or cynicism.

Robert L. Fried
The Passionate Teacher

Nobody forgets a good teacher.

Teacher Training Agency slogan

Tell Me Teacher

Teacher, teacher tell me true
Tell me what I ought to do!
Teacher, teacher, where's my book!
Tell me what I ought to look!
Tell me what to feel and how to think,
When to eat and what to drink.
Tell me what is good and what is bad,
When I'm happy and when I'm sad.
Tell me, tell me what to do.
Tell me, tell me what is true.
Make me learn and make me know,
Watch me closely as I come and go.
For I am small and I am weak,
Without your permission I cannot speak.
I cannot learn except by your decree,
Please, I beg you, give knowledge to me.
I am stupid and you are bright.
I am wrong and you are right.
I am bad and you are good.
I must do what you say I should.
Oh teacher, teacher, can't you see!
Look at what you've done to me!

H. Cole
'Tell me teacher', handout at Creative Problem-Solving Institute,
Creative Education Foundation, Buffalo, New York (1972)

Children esteem teachers who can explain things clearly; who are slightly strict rather than overly severe or permissive; scrupulously fair in their use of rewards and punishments; interested in them as individuals; and with a sense of humour not based on sarcasm or humiliation.

E.C. Wragg
The Art and Science of Teaching and Learning

Teachers teach in the way they do, not just because of the skills they have or have not learned. The ways they teach also are grounded in their backgrounds, their biographies, in the kind of teachers they have become. Their careers – their hopes and dreams, their opportunities and aspirations, are important for teachers' commitment, enthusiasm and morale. So too are relationships with their colleagues – either as supportive communities who work together in pursuit of common goals and continuous improvement, or as individuals working in isolation, with the insecurities that sometimes brings.

A. Hargreaves
Changing Teachers, Changing Times

It is what teachers think, what teachers believe, and what teachers do at the level of the classroom that ultimately shapes the kind of learning that young people get.

A. Hargreaves
Changing Teachers, Changing Times

Children and pupils see much more of us and in us and about us than we would like to imagine. They study us as they study their books, and often with considerably more interest. They read us. They see our body language and see through it; they spot where we scratch ourselves; they pick up the giveaway expressions in our eyes; they work out our values and smile at our evasions; they perceive our natures and assess our flash-points. No actor on the stage is more carefully studied.

Jonathan Smith
The Learning Game

A prime indicator of the effective school is one in which a high proportion of pupils have a good or vital relationship with one or more teachers. The ability to generate and sustain this good or vital relationship is a fundamentally important aspect of teaching quality.

There is a striking quality to fine classrooms. Pupils are caught up in learning; excitement abounds; and playfulness and seriousness blend easily because the purposes are clear, the goals sensible, and an unmistakable feeling of well being prevails.

Artist teachers achieve these qualities by knowing both their subject matter and their pupils; by guiding the learning with deft control – a control that itself is born out of perception, intuition, and creative impulse.

Louis Rubin
Artistry in Teaching

Teacher growth is closely related to pupil growth. Probably nothing within a school has more impact on students in terms of skills development, self-confidence, or classroom behaviour than the personal and professional growth of their teachers. The crux of teachers' professional growth, I feel, is the development of a capacity to observe and analyse the consequences for students of different teaching behaviour and materials, and to learn to make continuous modifications of teaching on the basis of cues students convey. Teachers also need to be able to relate their classroom behaviour to what other teachers are doing in their classrooms. Teachers think they do that. Many do, but many do not do it very systematically or regularly.

Roland S. Barth
Improving Schools from Within

Have you ever had a teacher? One who saw you as a raw but precious thing, a jewel, that with wisdom, could be polished to a proud shine?

If you are lucky enough to find your way to such teachers, you will always find your way back.

Anon

Teaching is not something one learns to do, once and for all, and then practises, problem free, for a lifetime, anymore than one knows how to have friends, and follows a static set of directions called 'friendships', through each encounter. Teaching depends on growth and development and is practised in dynamic situations that are never twice the same. Wonderful teachers, young and old, will tell of fascinating insights, new understandings, unique encounters with youngsters, the intellectual puzzle and the ethical dilemmas that provide a daily challenge. Teachers, above all, must stay alive to this.

William Ayers
To Teach

Teachers teach, but unless they learn constantly, they will be unable to perform their central role in a rapidly changing society. There is so much for them to learn.

They need to be able to develop new skills and understandings consistent with the latest research in education and psychology. Information technology impacts ever more profoundly on learning: they need to understand its impact and potential.

They need to keep up to date with their subject or subjects. They need also to understand the changing society in which we live so that they can guide or signpost their students into the inevitable uncertainties of the future.

Michael Barber
The Learning Game

There I found the secret of St Augustine's golden key, which though it be of gold is useless unless it fits the wards of the lock, and I found the wards I had to fit, the minds of those little street boys, very queer and tortuous affairs and I had to set about cutting and chipping myself into the shape of a wooden key, which however common it might look, should have the one merit of a key, the merit of unlocking the mind and opening the shut chambers of the heart.

Edward Thring
Theory and Practice of Teaching

Good teaching is not just a matter of being efficient, developing competence, mastering technique and possessing the right kind of knowledge. Good teaching also involves emotional work. It is infused with desire, pleasure, mission, creativity, challenge and joy. Good teaching is a profoundly emotional activity.

A. Hargreaves
Changing Teachers, Changing Times

It is teachers' passion for their subject that provides the basis for effective teaching and learning. These teachers use their subject expertise to engage students in meaningful learning experiences that embrace content, process and social climate. They create for and with their children opportunities to explore and build important areas of knowledge, and develop powerful tools for learning, within a supportive, collaborative and challenging classroom environment.

Robert L. Fried
The Passionate Teacher

More than anything else, more than expectations, passionate engagement or standards, teaching is about hope. Every child is the teacher's hope for the future. Education happens when hope exceeds expectation. Teaching is what makes the difference.

A. Hargreaves and M. Fullan
What's Worth Fighting for in Education?

A Good Teacher ...

is kind
is generous
listens to you
encourages you
has faith in you
keeps confidences
likes teaching children
likes teaching their subject
takes time to explain things
tells you when you're stuck

tells you how you are doing
allows you to have your say
doesn't give up on you
cares for your opinion
makes you feel clever
treats people equally
stands up for you
makes allowances
tells the truth
is forgiving

Descriptions by Year 8 students
Quoted in John MacBeath
Schools Must Speak for Themselves

Our task as teachers is to fill their pockets with the true confidence that comes from their completing a task they know to be significant and the quality of which we have successfully and positively identified.

Tim Brighouse
in *Birmingham Bulletin*, 1995

I have come to the frightening conclusion: I am the decisive element in the classroom. It is my personal approach that creates the climate. It is my daily mood that makes the weather. As a teacher I possess tremendous power to make a child's life miserable or joyous. I can be a tool of torture or an instrument of inspiration. I can humiliate or humour, hurt or heal. In all situations it is my response that decides whether a crisis will be escalated or de-escalated; a child humanised or dehumanised.

H.G. Ginott
Teacher and Child

One looks back with appreciation to the brilliant teachers, but with gratitude to those who touched our human feelings. The curriculum is so much necessary raw material but warmth is the vital element for the growing plant and for the soul of the child.

Carl Gustav Jung
Quoted in *International Education Quotations Encyclopaedia*

In the end, our talk must be of both the concrete and metaphysical aspects of teaching. The specific 'how-to's' and the inescapable 'whys' must come together in the practice and mingle in the example teachers set for their students. For what is powerful about teaching is that we convey to our students not only the wisdom and experience of the past but also the gift of unending discovery and limitless potential.

What is unique about being a teacher is that our students can learn as much from the questions we are still vigorously pursuing as from the wisdom we have garnered from years of passionate devotion to subjects and children.

Robert L. Fried
The Passionate Teacher

All of us want children to experience warmth, human interaction, the thrill of discovery, and solid grounding in essentials: reading, getting along with others, training in civic values …
Only a teacher, live in the classroom, can bring about this inspiration. This can't happen over a speaker, a television or a computer screen.

Clifford Stoll
Silicon Snake Oil

Appointing new teachers

Description

As part of the selection process, candidates are asked to teach a lesson before they are formally interviewed. They are told in advance what year and subject/topic they will be expected to teach and something about the ability range of the students. They are observed according to a set of criteria by one or two members of staff (not necessarily members of the interview panel) and the reports of the observer(s) are analysed and considered by the panel in the selection procedure. Feedback is also taken from the students.

Comment on impact

Recruitment of staff is one of the most important of management activities and it is therefore worth investing more care and time to select the best. Asking teachers to demonstrate their craft would seem to be a more effective way than relying solely on interview and references. It also has the benefit of involving other staff in the processes of classroom observation and staff selection, as well as students. Decisions taken on appointing new teachers are thus more widely shared and probably more successful. The interviewees also gain from the process in that it gives them a chance to find out more about what the school and its students are really like and to demonstrate skills that might not be revealed in the interview.

Teachers teaching teachers

Description
We have come across two variations of a single theme. Both are designed to encourage professional development discussion in the school.

The first school took three of their five INSET days and built time into half-hour sessions from 2.30pm to 7.30pm (with a meal ending at 9pm) for staff training. (They felt they could justify ending early on one day each half term.) The theme in Year 1 was teaching and learning. The other two days were used visiting in pairs or threes (it is important to avoid teachers doing it as singletons) to observe closely the practice in another school (for example questioning techniques, use of story, formative assessment and so on).

The second school does a 'late start' ('building societies do it for staff training, so can we') at 10.30am for pupils every fortnight and uses the 9am to 10.30am training session for professional development.

Both schools claim this as the factor which has changed the school the most – and for the better.

Comment on impact
One of the famous descriptions of a successful school (or department) is one where:

- Teachers talk about teaching
- Teachers observe each other teach
- Teachers plan, organise, monitor and evaluate their teaching together
- Teachers teach each other!

The schemes described in this butterfly clearly make sure that at least three of these criteria are met on a regular basis.

A staffroom teaching and learning notice board

Description

A special notice board in the staffroom just for articles, comments, cuttings, book reviews, butterflies, and so on related to teaching and learning. In one primary school all the staff take it in turn to provide materials for the notice board (which are changed every two weeks) and to talk about this during a staff meeting. In a secondary school, subject departments provide the material on a fortnightly rota, but on general teaching and learning issues, not just their subject discipline.

Comment on impact

The notice board generates interest and discussion about teaching and learning informally and formally, as it is in the staffroom. These notice boards usually highlight key articles from the *Times Educational Supplement*, education magazines and other sources, as well as books that would aid staff development. Sometimes there is also a 'butterfly of the week' displayed.

Chapter 4

Learning

> If pupils don't learn the way we teach, perhaps we
> should teach the way they learn.
>
> Howard Gardner
> *The Unschooled Mind*

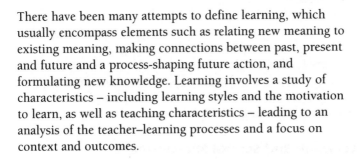

There have been many attempts to define learning, which
usually encompass elements such as relating new meaning to
existing meaning, making connections between past, present
and future and a process-shaping future action, and
formulating new knowledge. Learning involves a study of
characteristics – including learning styles and the motivation
to learn, as well as teaching characteristics – leading to an
analysis of the teacher–learning processes and a focus on
context and outcomes.

Several researchers and writers, as the following quotations
illustrate, have referred to 'learnacy' or 'learning power',
variously defined as resourcefulness in the sense of being able
to learn in different ways, resilience in the readiness and
persistence in learning, reflectiveness in being able to become
more strategic about learning, reciprocity in being able to learn
alone and with others, and responsiveness in being able to
adapt to different styles of learning. Others have stressed the

importance of understanding multiple intelligences and the particular importance of emotional intelligence in learning how to learn. In learning we always have to pay regard to the 'cognitive' and 'affective' domains, explained beautifully by Sir Alec Clegg as 'loaves' and 'hyacinths': 'the loaves are mainly concerned with facts and their manipulation, and they draw on the intellect. The hyacinths are concerned with a child's loves, hates, fears, enthusiasm and antipathies, with his courage, his compassion and his confidence.'[1]

When it is truly effective education gives young people exposure to a wider range of contexts and role models for learning, along with experience of genuine responsibility. Learning takes place everywhere, using a broad range of resources – cultural, social, financial and physical – and we need to be aware of the entire landscape of learning which combines the rigours of the best professional instruction with the flexibility and motivational power of work, community and collaborative learning.

As far as schools are concerned, learning will be influenced by the form of organization, the style of management and the climate of relationships, although schools that promote effective learning will develop approaches which share the characteristics of learning out of school, such as first-hand, self-assessed learning in a 'real' context.

Learning and school improvement

The quality of learning is at the heart of school improvement. In successful schools the staff have thought through what constitutes effective learning in their particular context in order to raise the achievement of all students and put into place appropriate processes and practices. They will be aware of the dangers of young people's learning being dominated by

----

[1] A. Clegg, *About our Schools*, Blackwell (1980).

judgements of ability which can profoundly affect their self-esteem and sense of identity; and that students learn very quickly about their standing in comparison with their peers relative to their supposed ability and which category they belong to, in terms of 'more able', 'average' and 'less able'. This kind of learning is often reinforced daily through many different kinds of experiences and it takes a conscious effort to practise 'learning without limits', so that young people's school experiences are not all organized and structured on the basis of judgements of ability.

Where schools are 'learning enriched' all members of the organization are involved in a process of continuous review and evaluation and believe that they are part of a professional learning community. Such schools have an agreed policy on learning and teaching, which covers the central issues of personalized learning, learning styles, assessment for learning and the use of learning resources.

Personalized learning

Personalized learning is about helping every child and young person to do better, which means tailoring education to individual needs, interests and aptitudes so as to fulfil their potential, and giving them the motivation to be independent, lifelong learners. For schools it means a professional ethos that accepts and assumes that every child comes into the classroom with a different knowledge base and set of skills, as well as varying aptitudes and aspirations.

The key components of personalized learning are usually taken to be effective teaching and learning strategies, requiring a wide range of whole-class, group and individual teaching, along with learning and ICT strategies, curriculum entitlement and choice that delivers a breadth of study, personal relevance and flexible learning pathways through the education system; assessment for learning, to identify every student's learning needs; school organization so as best to support high quality teaching and learning; and strong partnerships beyond the school to remove barriers to learning and to support student well-being. Schools will recognize this agenda as trying to do their best for every child and young person by adapting schooling to meet the needs of the individual rather than forcing the individual to fit the system.

Most schools would claim that they give students individual attention, but those that are working hard on personalized education have realized that there is a lot more that they can do, particularly in allowing students opportunities to work at their own pace. Choice is also an important part of personalized learning, particularly in secondary schools, with the building of individual learning pathways. However, the constraints of syllabus, curriculum and assessment can make it very difficult to offer a truly personalized form of learning, although there have been some innovative approaches through the benefits of workforce remodelling and more effective use of ICT. In the last analysis 'the curriculum' must appeal to the individual or the group. In the end, the successful learner is engaged in the curriculum which the teacher has tailored to the world. For example, teachers have rightly criticized the 'one size fits all' National Curriculum and literacy and numeracy strategies because they are overprescriptive and deskill teachers by discouraging them from bringing their own views to the curriculum, even at the margin.

It also needs to be recognized that the school day and the school year provide only a small percentage of available learning time. That's why the suspended timetable involving a 'day' or a 'week' of learning is so important to successful learning.

To succeed in their hope of enhancing learning and achievement, schools must find new allies and build new sorts of connections to the community of which they are a part. One of the first key steps is to build an effective home and community curriculum based mainly on learning partnerships with parents and carers, remembering that they are co-educators of children in parallel with teachers. Thus home–school contact to support learning at home is co-operation with the school, an emphasis on self-directed learning, and indeed opportunities provided by the school for parents to enhance their own learning, sometimes gaining formal qualifications or the confidence to learn with their own children. Other important agencies in the community which support learning include services and businesses through which students can gain greater economic awareness and an appreciation of the nature of citizenship. Businesses can continue support in terms of learning mentors or helping with Young Enterprise Programmes and through Education Business Partnerships.

The most important attribute that schools can give students is the ability to learn on their own and to take responsibility for their own learning. While this can be encouraged through the formal curriculum in terms of flexible learning and independent learning, the provision of curriculum enrichment and extension opportunities creates a real opportunity to prepare for lifelong learning, whether through traditional extra-curricular activities – such as sport, drama, chess and other clubs and societies – or through study opportunities provided before and after school by breakfast clubs or at weekends and holidays – such as courses and residential learning experiences, Easter revision courses, summer schools or study extension with organizations such as the Children's University or Gifted and Talented Centres. Curriculum enrichment and extension and learning beyond the school allows for the greater personalization of learning and extra opportunities to improve motivation and build self-esteem.

Learning styles

The concept of learning styles has become a cornerstone of good practice, although not without its critics. The most commonly used system in schools is the VAK model of classification, which divides children into visual, auditory or kinesthetic learners: those who like to look, those who like to listen and those who learn best through physical activity, sometimes called 'active learners'. Most learning styles analysis relies on self-assessment questionnaires completed by children. This has obvious defects. Many school activities are not purely visual, auditory or kinesthetic but a mixture of all three. Even if we accept that children learn in different ways, most teachers agree that a preferred learning style is simply an acquired habit and that children need to experience other styles. Most schools that embrace the concept of learning styles try to encourage teachers to make lessons accessible to all students by including visual, auditory and kinesthetic elements. They believe that it is equally important for teachers to analyse their own style of learning and teaching. Most teachers, they argue, allow their own style to become their habitual teaching style – to the detriment of those students who learn in different ways.

The danger with other rigid classifications of children's learning preferences is that children will be labelled and forced into a narrow view of their own abilities. However, some mechanisms for assessing learning styles take a more holistic view and look at a wide range of issues under the heading of Learning Styles. For example the Learning Style Analysis profiles promoted by the publisher of this book (NCE)[2] are based on a wide series of questions grouped under categories that are brain-based, sensory, physical, environmental, social and attitudinal. These profiles (which are accessible online) are based on the research work of Professors Dunn and Dunn of New York in the 1980s, and now developed into electronic format by Professor Barbara Prashnig of Auckland, New Zealand. The outcomes or profiles avoid labelling children by describing preferences, non-preferences and flexibilities in the spectrum of issues involved.

----

[2] The Learning Styles Analysis website is accessible at http://www.networkcontinuum.co.uk.

Nevertheless, it seems that learning style models are still a huge simplification of the complex way in which children process information. However, the debate over learning styles has at least encouraged teachers to examine their own practice and explore a wider repertoire of teaching strategies. Perhaps instead of talking about learning styles we should talk about learning skills and the provision of an environment most suitable for learning, whether that is individual, group or class working, the availability of learning technologies or aural stimulation.

Assessment for learning

Personalized learning is closely linked to the assessment of students, in the sense that you cannot tailor learning unless you know about student progress. But the emphasis here is on assessment *for* learning, rather than assessment *of* learning, so that students can improve on their achievements and make progress. There are different ways of achieving this but the rationale is always the same: clear evidence about how to drive up individual attainment; clear feedback for and from students so there is clarity on what they need to improve and how best they can do so. New technologies makes individual target setting possible, tracking students' progress through the school not just on test scores but on attendance, behaviour and achievement generally, something that can be shared with students and their parents to get them closely involved in the learning process.

Learning technologies

Making the most effective use of learning resources is a great challenge for schools and integral to any discussion about learning and teaching. There are key policy issues that need to be worked through, including individual access to information technology; the personalization of learning; the design of classrooms and learning areas, including the library/resource centre. The long-term development of student responsibility and independent learning requires an institutional approach, as does the development of the role of the teacher in managing resource-based learning. Teachers need to be seen increasingly as managers of learning and less as presenters of information. In this context the use and management of learning technologies is fundamental to effective learning and achievement.

Good schools will have a strategic view on the place of ICT across the curriculum, and improved access for all learners. When students come to school many, though not of course the disadvantaged few, leave the wired-up world of their homes where access to television, video and computers is commonplace, to enter a building where ICT learning resources are still not extensively employed in everyday learning, although new technologies are making considerable headway. Thankfully, in a society and economy where ICT is transforming the way we live and earn our living, all schools are radically re-examining how students should be learning, not least because of all that we know about how students learn at different rates and in different ways. Schools of this new millennium will have a vision of how to use shared intelligence rather than relying simply on teacher intelligence, although they will never forget that good teaching inspires the best learning. Full use of the new learning technologies helps teachers and support staff to create a learning environment where students can build actions and create knowledge, something that can be carried on within the home and the community. Learning through ICT, including email addresses for staff and students, will enhance and enrich the curriculum and its assessment, offering new and exciting opportunities for individual learners to access a wider range of quality learning programmes and materials. A good school takes full advantage of the fact that everybody in the learning community can create, receive, collect and share text, images and sounds on a vast range of topics, in ways more stimulating, richer and more time-efficient than ever before.

Learner characteristics are not fixed: previous experiences and previous competence and beliefs influence present learning. Learning can occur through multiple channels and through different learning styles. Learners vary in their beliefs about success and in their motivation for learning. The school, as the key site of institutional learning, models effective learning by encouraging the personalization of learning within a climate of high expectations, joint learning and shared responsibility for learning. Schools that themselves become professional learning communities are better able to connect with learning out of school, so that their children and young people can become effective, enthusiastic and independent learners committed to lifelong learning and better able to cope with the demands of adult life.

Quotations

Learning is the whole business of the school: it deserves to be in the forefront of the minds and conversations of everyone in school who nowadays need to guard against displacing learning by managerial or organisational topics.

Tim Brighouse and David Woods
How to Improve Your School

Learning does not take place in isolation from children's feelings. Being emotionally literate is as important for learning as instruction in maths or reading.

Daniel Goleman
Emotional Intelligence

All children are gifted ...
Some just open their packages sooner than others.

Anon

The important thing is not to stop questioning.

Albert Einstein
The World as I See It

Live as if you were to die tomorrow, learn as if you were to live forever.

Mohandas K. Gandhi
Quoted in *Grey's Essential Miscellany for Teachers*

Learn as though you would never be able to master it; hold it as though you would be in fear of losing it.

Confucius

Emotional literacy implies an extended mandate for schools, taking up the slack in terms of socialising children. This daunting task requires that teachers go beyond their traditional mission and that people in the community become more involved with schools. In this sense, emotional literacy goes hand in hand with education for character, for moral development, and for citizenship.

Emotional competence may be decisive in determining the extent to which any given child or teenager is undone by economic or family forces or finds a core of resistance to survive them.

Daniel Goleman
Emotional Intelligence

The purpose of the curriculum is not to cover but to uncover.

Anon

Instead of a national curriculum for education, what is really needed is an individual curriculum for every child.

Charles B. Handy
The Age of Unreason

… one had to cram all this stuff into one's mind whether one liked it or not; this coercion had such a deterring effect that after I had gained the final examinations, I found the consideration of any scientific problems distasteful to me for a whole year. It is in fact nothing short of a miracle that the modern methods of instruction have not yet entirely stamped out the holy curiosity of enquiry, for this delicate little plant arising from stimulation stands mainly in need of freedom without which it goes to wrack and ruin without fail. It is a very grave mistake to think that the enjoyment of learning can be promoted by coercion and a sense of duty.

Albert Einstein
The World as I See It

The right way to feed these Things is to give them a Liking and Inclination to what you propose to them to be learned and that will engage their Industry and Appreciation … Thus much for learning to read which let him never be driven to, nor chid for: cheat him into it if you can but make it not a Business for him! tis better to be a year later before he can read than he should in his way get an Aversion to Learning.

John Locke
Some Thoughts Concerning Education

What we want is to see the child in pursuit of knowledge, and not knowledge in pursuit of the child.

Attributed to George Bernard Shaw

We all teach and learn, all our lives.

Gilbert Highet
The Art of Teaching

There is an alternative, a second kind of learning … This is learning that is free from the constraints of being labelled top, middle or bottom, fast or slow, free from the wounding consciousness of being treated as someone who can aspire at best to only limited achievements. Learning without limits becomes possible when young people's school experiences are not organised and structured on the basis of judgements of ability.

Hart, Dixon, Drummond and McIntyre
Learning without Limits

One of the great tragedies of the last hundred years has been our failure as a nation to take on the essential concept of human educability and thereby challenge the idea that children are born with a given quota of 'intelligence' which remains constant both during childhood and adult life.

Clive Chitty
'IQ, Racism and the Eugenics Movement'

The 6 Es of Organisational Success

These are the things which trigger energy, excitement, enthusiasm, effort, effervescence and enterprise. Everyone is full of 'e' in all its forms. The trick is to release that 'e' – the excitement as well as the effort, the enthusiasm as well as the energy. The more organisations can match these personal 'e' factors and bubble with them the more successful and fun they will be.

Charles B. Handy
Inside Organisations

Imagine oneself on a ship sailing across an unknown sea, to an unknown destination. An adult would be desperate to know where he is going. But a child only knows he is going to school ... the chart is neither available nor understandable to him – very quickly, the daily life on board ship becomes all important. The daily chores, the demands, the inspections, become the reality, not the voyage, not the destination.

Mary A. White
The Experience of Schooling

Qualities which children need to do well at school – 4 Cs

Confidence
Curiosity
Communication
Co-operation

US National Center for Infant Programs

Those who are designated 'bright' know by that very fact they are being complimented and credited with a valuable attribute. The 'less able' understand that they lack the very quality on which the school sets most store; a sense of failure tends to permeate the whole personality, leaving a residue of powerlessness and hopelessness.

D.H. Hargreaves
The Challenge for the Comprehensive School

The 5 Rs of Learnacy

Resourcefulness
Remembering
Resilience
Reflectiveness
Responsiveness

B. Lucas
Discover your Hidden Talents

It should be the first duty of a school for life to help the young person build up an 'intelligence profile', then to encourage him or her to develop the preferred set of those intelligences, and to work out how best to employ them. This will provide the basis for that self-confidence without which little learning can occur.

Charles Handy
The Hungry Spirit

There is, in fact, no teaching without learning.

Paolo Freire
Pedagogy of the Oppressed

Learning … that reflective activity which enables the learner to draw upon previous experience to understand and evaluate the present, so as to shape future action and formulate new knowledge.

John Abbott
Learning makes Sense

The ability to cope with change, learning as much as possible with each encounter, is the generic capacity needed for the 21st century.

Michael Fullan
Change Forces with a Vengeance

In times of change learners inherit the earth whilst the learned find themselves beautifully equipped to deal with a world that no longer exists.

Eric Hoffer
Vanguard Management

Anything worth learning takes time to learn, and time to teach.

Gilbert Highet
The Art of Teaching

The illiterate of the 21st Century will not be those who cannot read or write, but those who cannot learn, unlearn and relearn. Our students need to be information literate, lifelong learners.

Alvin Toffler
Information Studies

Ability is not a fixed property; there is a huge variability in how you perform. People who have a sense of self-efficacy bounce back from failure.

Albert Bandura

Learning is not compulsory but neither is survival.

W.E. Deming
Out of the Crisis

People who are unable to motivate themselves must be content with mediocrity, no matter how impressive their other talents.

Andrew Carnegie

Curiosity is one of the most permanent and certain characteristics of a rigorous intellect.

Samuel Johnson
The Rambler

Significant learning contains the logical and the intuitive, the intellect and the feelings, the concept and the experience, the idea and the meaning.

Carl Rogers and H.J. Freiberg
Freedom to Learn

Focused intelligence, the ability to acquire and apply knowledge and know-how, is the new source of wealth. Education is the crucial key to future wealth, but it is a key which takes a long time to shape and a long time to turn. The good news is that everyone can be intelligent in some way or can get intelligent. Intelligence has many faces, all of them useful, all of them potential property in the new world of intelligence. We need to have a clear idea of our best intelligences and learn to make the most of them. It should be the first duty of any school to discover one's intelligences and deploy them.

Charles B. Handy
The Empty Raincoat

Tell me, and I will forget.
Show me, and I may remember.
Involve me, and I will understand

Confucius

Even though a high IQ is no guarantee of prosperity, prestige, or happiness in life, our schools and our culture fixate on academic abilities, ignoring emotional intelligence, a set of traits – some might call it character – that also matters immensely for our personal destiny. Emotional life is a domain that, as surely as math or reading, can be handled with greater or lesser skill, and requires its unique set of competencies … emotional aptitude is a meta-ability, determining how well we can use whatever other skills we have.

Daniel Goleman
Emotional Intelligence

Children may be 20% of the population but they are 100% of the future.

David Tyack
The One Best System

At school I knew one thing for sure, that every problem in the world had already been solved by someone. The answers to many of them were in the teacher's head or in the back of their text books. If they were not, then they were bound to be in someone else's head or in someone else's book.

The message I carried away was clear – if you meet with an unfamiliar problem, find the expert, and ask them. It was a crippling message. Until I unlearnt it I was unaware of my own capabilities and sometimes doubting whether I had any. I had acquired for myself the assumption of stupidity when what I really needed was the habit of curiosity.

Charles B. Handy
Inside Organisations

Sometimes I look about me with a feeling of complete dismay. In the confusion that afflicts the world today, I see disrespect for the very values of life. Beauty is all around us, but how many seem to see nothing. Each second we live is a new and unique moment of the universe; a moment that will never be again. And what do we teach our children? We teach them that 2 + 2 makes 4, and that Paris is the capital of France. When will we also teach them what they are?

We should say to each of them: do you know what you are? You are a marvel. You are unique. In the entire world there is no other child exactly like you. In the millions of years that have passed, there has never been another child like you. And look at your body – what a wonder it is. Your legs, your arms, your cunning fingers, and the way you move. You may become a Shakespeare, a Michelangelo, a Beethoven. And when you grow up, can you then harm another who is, like you, a marvel? You must cherish one another. You must work – we must all work – to make this world worthy of its children.

Pablo Casals
Joys and Sorrows

One hundred

The child is made of one hundred.
The child has a hundred languages,
a hundred hands, a hundred thoughts
a hundred ways of thinking,
of playing, of speaking.
A hundred, always a hundred
ways of listening,
of marvelling, of loving,
a hundred joys,
for singing and understanding,
a hundred worlds to discover
a hundred worlds to invent
a hundred worlds to dream.
The child has a hundred languages
(and a hundred, hundred, hundred more)
but they steal the ninety-nine.

The school and the culture
separate the head from the body.
They tell the child:
to think without hands
to do without head
to listen and not to speak
to understand without joy
to love and to marvel
only at Easter and Christmas.
They tell the child:
to discover the world already there
and of the hundred they steal the
ninety-nine.
They tell the child:
that work and play
reality and fantasy
science and imagination
sky and earth

reason and dream
are things that do not belong
together.
And thus they tell the child
that the hundred is not there.

The child says:
No way. The hundred is there.

Loris Malaguzzi

Learning is like moving upstream; not to
advance is to drop back.

Chinese proverb
Cited in *The International Education Quotations Encyclopaedia*

If, as it is said, the Battle of Waterloo was won
on the playing fields of Eton, the great
discoveries and new options of the 21st century
may well be won in the nurseries of the 20th.

Peter Kline
The Everyday Genius

Learning how to learn goes well beyond study and information skills. It involves developing thinking skills and problem solving but also includes being creative and generating new ideas. It includes personal qualities such as honesty and self esteem or what has been referred to as 'emotional intelligence'. In fact, learning to learn is very close to learning to be.

Daniel Goleman
Emotional Intelligence

Continuous learning for everyone is central to the notion of the intelligent school.

MacGilchrist, Myers and Reed
The Intelligent School

In nearly every student there is a five year old 'unschooled mind' struggling to get out and express itself.

Howard Gardner
The Unschooled Mind

But no-one can unlock a door without a key. The world is full of locked doors. Every child is a locked door. But where are the keys? Where is there any distinct conviction that any key is wanted? That such an article as a key to mind exists? The sloppy idea of education which prevails, reduced to shape and practice, means a set of trucks all in a row, memory trucks with navvies pitching ballast into them against time. Or not doing so as the case may be. But loading up other people with fact is not training minds. One more point demands notice. There are not only no keys but the present system prevents keys being made. A key is adapted to fit intricacies and to wind in and out of queer passages. The successful scholar is a man who has run through his work smoothly and found the least obstacles. And these are the men who are selected to deal with the greatest number of obstacles and difficulties.

Edward Thring
Headmaster of Uppingham School
Letter to *The Times* (1886)

Each child's resources and strengths must be the deciding factors in establishing an educational programme. [Rather than look for weaknesses] we would do better to look for strengths and recognise that these will be different for different children. Differences offer hope because they provide the possibility of alternative routes for development, educational and personal fulfilment. We would rejoice in them and capitalise on them. They are, after all, the very stuff of life.

K.J. Connolly
'In Praise of Difference'

We have entered a new century in which learning will define our lives as never before. Whether we succeed and prosper, as individuals or as a country or fail to progress and fall behind, will depend on our knowledge and skills, abilities and understanding.

David Blunkett, MP
Raising Aspirations in the 21st Century

Like WW2 evacuees,
New pupils arrive in new classrooms
Responding to the annual clarion call
To a new school year, a fresh start.

They too bring their baggage,
Not in cardboard boxes and string
But wrapped up in experience –
Of home with its support of apathy, stability or tension;
Of school with friends or enemies, in teachers and
classmates;
Of encouragement and derision, raised expectations and
thwarted dreams;
Of elation and despair, with success and failure;
Of tests with their annual boost to confidence,
Or their destruction of self-esteem.

They too bring a label,
Not tied to a lapel
With name and destination,
But one just as tangible, just as narrow in objective:
One that decrees that the bearer is
Level 5, Level 4, Level 3 or Working towards Level 3
Everyone knows – teachers, parents … and children,
Most of whom are not thick enough
Not to know or care.

Alan Day

Oh bring back higher standards

Oh bring back higher standards – the pencil and the cane
– if we want education then we must have some pain.

Oh bring us back all the gone days

Yes, bring back all the past … let's put them all in rows
again – so we can see who's last.

Let's label all the good ones (the ones like you and me)
and make them into prefects – like prefects used to be.

We'll put them on the honours board … as honours
ought to be, and write their name in burnished script –
for all the world to see.

We'll have them back in uniform, we'll have them doff
their caps, and learn what manners really are … for
decent kind of chaps!

… So let's label all the good ones, we'll call them 'A's'
and 'B's' – and we'll parcel up all the useless ones and
call them 'C's' and 'D's' … We'll even have an 'E' lot! …
an 'F' or 'G' maybe!! … so they can know they're useless,
… and not as good as me.

For we've got to have the stupid –

And we've got to have the poor

Because – if we don't have them … well … what are
prefects for?

Peter Dixon
Grow your own Poems

Butterflies

Sharing good practice

Description

We firmly believe in the maxim that 'the biggest and most underused resource teachers have is each other', but realized that we had to do something more than merely exhort colleagues to share good ideas. We formally introduced, as a matter of policy, 'Sharing good practice' as the first item on the agenda of every departmental, middle management and staff meeting.

One member of the SLT was responsible for organizing which teacher was to present, on what topic, at which meeting, thereby ensuring that there was a broad range of contributions, from different subject disciplines. All the slots were short, a maximum of 10 minutes, and colleagues were encouraged to be as interactive with their peers as they would be with their students.

Many of the presentations are subsequently published in the staff bulletin, so that they are available to all teachers.

Comment on impact

The impact has been very powerful indeed. Staff come away from meetings with a practical idea they can use in their lessons the next day and it has been an excellent way to initiate cross-subject and cross-discipline working arrangements.

Another remarkable development is that although it began with SLT and AST leading the presentations, now a second year teacher would be leading a session for 35 middle managers: in the school, everyone's a learner!

High leverage in terms of staff development and the improvement of teaching and learning.

Proximal learning

Description
The school agreed that it was more effective to have one whole-school focus for lesson observations undertaken by members of the middle and senior team. Structured talk in pairs or proximal learning was an early focus. Training on what made the proximal work effective was provided for all staff at a whole-school INSET. It was then agreed that every lesson, in every subject, for the term would have a slot for paired talk. All observations would focus only on proximal work so teachers would really get this right. For example proximal work could form part of a starter or plenary – for example talk together for two minutes on five effects of tropical storms you learned in the lesson – or a longer exercise, discussing a talk first and then completing a written element, often on a shared piece of paper. Giving a set amount of time for the proximal task is key. Students experienced this approach across the school and all soon became skilled at taking part.

Comment on impact
All students could do this. It worked powerfully as it was developing oral work across the whole school. Having one whole-school focus for observations ensured the initiative – small as it was – became quickly and very effectively embedded into the school. All staff now talk about 'putting some proximal into the lesson'. Staff share proximal activities that work particularly well. New staff observe lessons to see proximal work in action, as it is such a key feature of the way staff teach. As a development it cost almost nothing and had a major impact. For boys (and reluctant writers) it enabled action first and writing second – it gave even weaker students things to say. Working in pairs and not small groups meant no student could 'hide' and opt out. All had to be engaged in the task. The quality of speaking skills improved very significantly in a very short time across the age, gender and ability range. High leverage in improving teaching and learning.

Topping up a school staff's 'intellectual capacity' and keeping a lively focus on teaching and learning

Description

One school has set aside one of its five INSET days to be taken in term time. It then arranged staff visits, in 'twos', 'threes' and 'fours', to schools chosen because of their interesting practice. The visits have both a 'subject' and 'whole school' purpose. So the Art Department, for example, might be working on vocational GCSE option courses but also on the visits they might look at, for example, the use of questioning techniques or interactive whiteboards. Science staff would also look at general issues but, for their own subject, be looking at the piloting in another school of the 'Science for the 21st Century' GCSE course. (These are just examples, of course.) The collective follow-up will be at faculty meetings and the group looking at the learning, teaching and assessment policy of the school.

Comment on impact

The school's leadership team clearly made a key decision to introduce this rather large butterfly! They were anxious to top up the school staff's 'intellectual capacity' and at the same time keep a focus on teaching, learning and assessment.

Chapter 5

School improvement and evaluation

> The greatest danger is not that our aim is too high –
> but that it is too low and we reach it.
>
> Michelangelo

School improvement has witnessed an enormous growth of research and writing in the last 20 years or so, as the accompanying quotations illustrate.

In a previous publication (*How to Improve Your School*, 1999) we sought to offer a grammar of school improvement, to provide a common language of analysis, discussion and debate relating to the parallel worlds of school improvement and school effectiveness. The nouns were the key factors of school effectiveness, the verbs the processes of school improvement, the adjectives the descriptors of successful practices, and the punctuation and the adverbial clauses were the small and large interventions of school improvement. The chapters were the planned changes, over time, which make up the melodies and rhythms of school improvement.

In this brief overview of school improvement we seek to concentrate on the process of school improvement, and in particular high-leverage interventions that can make a significant difference to the life and work of a school. As far as the processes of school improvement are concerned we still stand by the seven that we originally identified, although modified slightly to allow for further developments in research and practice. These are:

The exercise of leadership.
The practice of management and organization.
The practice of teaching and learning and assessment.
The creation of an environment most fit for learning.
The practice of staff development.
The exercise of collective review and self-evaluation.
The involvement of parents and the community.

We often use the metaphor of 'the journey' to describe the improvement processes in schools and we believe that these seven processes taken as a whole make up a map of school improvement and a compass by which to navigate the journey, so that we travel not as nomads but as pilgrims. In other chapters and sets of quotations in this book we cover the areas of leadership, management, teaching and learning, and with them take into account the practice of staff development and the creation of an environment most suitable for learning – including the involvement of parents and the community – saying something about how these processes can be developed to increase school effectiveness and examining findings from school practice and researchers. However, before commenting upon these interventions and change processes, which seem to be the most effective in driving forward school improvement, we need to say much more about collective review and school self-evaluation in a time when all schools are required by Ofsted to complete and continually review a school evaluation form.

The striking characteristic of the 'moving' school as opposed to the 'stuck' school is that it has a culture that sustains critical reflection and enquiry coupled with a determination to secure continuous improvement. Moving schools have a high consensus about their values and objectives, they have considerable certainty, high commitment, cohesiveness and collaboration, and they are learning enriched.

Evaluation comes from the will to collect evidence and debate implications, and schools may adopt different strategies to achieve this although everybody will need to take account of the new Ofsted Framework to make judgements about the quality of education in their own school. There are many different approaches to school self-evaluation (see the box overleaf).

Most schools use a combination of such approaches to the key questions:

HOW DO WE KNOW? Everything depends here on the *quality* of evidence a school is able to present and how it seeks to collect evidence as a matter of everyday routine.

HOW GOOD IS OUR SCHOOL? The key aspects of school life and performance will need to be judged on a four-point scale of outstanding, good, satisfactory and inadequate – something schools will get right if they have fully developed their reflective intelligence and are confident about their capacity to identify strengths and weaknesses.

WHAT MUST WE DO TO IMPROVE?

In such a self-evaluating culture there will be supportive and knowledgeable leadership, reflective dialogue, openness to improvement, a collective focus on student learning, collaboration and norms of sharing, and a celebration of

APPROACHES TO SCHOOL SELF-EVALUATION

The *checklist/audit approach*, where a school carries out an audit against a list of questions generated by the school, LEA, DfES or Ofsted which seek to identify strengths and weaknesses with a view to establishing priorities for improvement.

The *performance management approach*, using strategies for the appraisal of school staff, to bring the focus of evaluation closer to where it really matters: the quality of teaching and learning.

The *stakeholder approach*, which involves the school in surveying the views and attitudes towards the school of students, parents and other interested parties.

The *benchmarking approach*, where the performance of the school is compared to that of other schools through performance and value-added tables, PANDAs, or other agencies such as the Fischer Family Trust or a Local Family of Schools data set such as that provided by the London Challenge.

The *Quality Mark approach*, where schools seek external recognition of aspects of their work and standards such as Investors in People, Artsmark, Sportsmark, the Healthy Schools standard, or the achievement of a particular status through the DfES such as Specialist College, Training School or Extended School.

The *case study approach*, where the school's capacity for improvement is reflected in its strong culture of professional reflection and its case studies of success, some of which are published externally, but all of which bear testimony to an active, reflective, intelligence geared to school improvement.

leading-edge practice. The school becomes a professional learning community which builds in time for collective enquiry and reviewing evidence, which uses action research to improve practice, and where school teachers are encouraged to collaborate by learning with and from each other. The school as an organization is a learning system and learns its way forward, going beyond the normal system of identifying the problem, analysing causes and solutions, and action planning, to 'appreciative enquiry' – appreciating the best of what is, envisioning what might be the best and promoting a dialogue for new knowledge, thinking and practice.

In terms of interventions and change processes we need to remind ourselves that context is crucial, with variables including the background of the students (race, socio-economic status, faith), the community the school serves (from affluent areas to those with considerable social and economic challenges) and where the school currently is in the local 'pecking order', with consequences for admissions and budgets.

In terms of school improvement every school is at a different point in the trajectory of its journey; it may be on the way up or declining or simply coasting, or, to confuse matters further, it may be a mixture of all three according to the effectiveness of particular parts of the school. Prescriptions for school improvement thus run the risk of either being so general as to be something to which we can all subscribe or, at the other extreme, being so detailed and explicit that they do not connect to a particular school's context and can therefore be too easily dismissed as irrelevant. Nevertheless, we believe that all schools, whether through critical self-evaluation or external consultancy, can identify for themselves those practices which can yield the highest leverage, rather than spending a lot of time and effort on practice whose pay-off is paltry.

We can make a useful distinction here between the 'adverbial clauses' of school improvement and very small interventions or 'punctuations'. We call the latter 'butterflies' after the work on chaos theory which has produced the concept of the 'butterfly effect', which teaches us that tiny differences in input can quickly become overwhelming differences in output. In weather, for example, it is argued that butterflies stirring the air today in Beijing can transform weather systems next month in New York. We have previously edited collections of such 'butterflies' taken from schools in both Birmingham (1999) and London (2005) and identified a school 'butterfly effect' (see the box opposite).

Through this process the school will continue to put into effect a number of small interventions that are capable of transforming behaviour and practice. Most importantly, however, the staff will be encouraged to be continually engaged in thinking, speculating and reflecting on the processes of school improvement and the subtleties of change. We believe that all schools, whatever their circumstances, can build collections of butterflies which make up a set of shared practices that can change behaviour at every level of the organization. We know some schools which introduce butterflies at occasional morning briefings and have a butterfly board display. The best butterflies will affect most processes of school improvement and make an immediate and disproportiate difference to the climate and culture of the school. Of course, some quotations in the hands of school leaders can also be butterflies of inspiration to those who encounter them for the first time, and for whom they have resonance. That's the purpose of this collection.

The 'adverbial clauses' of school improvement are those larger, critical interventions which are part of an integrated and focused programme of change which may take up to a year to implement and perhaps longer to embed thoroughly in the culture of the school. They are designed to make a distinct difference to

THE SCHOOL BUTTERFLY EFFECT

Describe and define to the staff what butterflies are and how they can effect change.

↓

Design an appropriate pro forma to capture the essence of these small interventions, relating their effect to the seven processes of school improvement and their impact on changing practices.

↓

Initially ask all staff for three contributions that may affect teaching and learning practices.

↓

Publish these as a collection for dissemination and debate and decide on those to be collectively implemented.

↓

Build the collection of butterflies into the culture of the school by starting all staff meetings with the description of a butterfly, and asking for further contributions on specific themes such as raising achievement, and promoting a positive ethos.

↓

Extend the process to include governors and the wider school community.

↓

Evaluate the cumulative effect of these many small interventions on the effectiveness of the school.

↓

Continue to publish and disseminate collections of new butterflies, while reviewing, and if necessary modifying, those that are already being practised.

previous practice. They will usually have a significant impact on teachers' behaviour as reflective professionals, on student development and learning, and on whole-school culture, and they need to be monitored and evaluated appropriately. Critical interventions, as major case studies of educational change, form part of the action research of the school and ought to be written up and published with an eye to disseminating good practice and identifying future developments.

There are, we believe, even allowing for a wide range of contexts, some critical interventions which are more rather than less likely to increase success, and these are set out briefly below.

Raising the standard

Raising the standard involves review and analysis of achievement data to examine critically anomalies, patterns and trends so that informed priorities and targets can be established. Data on the performance of schools are now very sophisticated, with a range of benchmarked information being available from the DfES and Ofsted; and the school's own self-evaluation form calls for a rigorous analysis of the data sets and the setting of appropriate priorities. Schools can critically intervene in this area by setting targets for taking action at various fixed points to raise educational standards, not just for the school as a whole, but for particular groups and, crucially, for individual students. A school can only be considered effective if it promotes progress beyond what would be expected, given prior attainment and development factors, for all its students – and school effectiveness research shows how important are high expectations in raising standards of achievement. The techniques employed to raise standards are many and varied but they are all based on a rigorous analysis of the data, including benchmarked comparisons, continual assessment of student progress and review of targets, and the consistency of practice across all teachers and support staff, and on-going monitoring and evaluation strategies. Too often detailed analysis of data is left to the senior leadership team when, if it is to make a real difference, all those who teach students have to understand their full personal profiles and individual targets and what they can contribute to their achievement.

Personalized learning

This leads on naturally to what the DfES refers to as '*personalized learning*' and its application in a whole-school setting, whereby schools have considered much more each student's individual needs and how they learn to learn, the assessment of that learning, the part that new techniques can play, new curriculum designs and the development of individual learning plans for each student backed up by appropriate coaching and mentoring alongside advice and guidance. They know that their students will benefit considerably from having a programme of one-to-one tutoring, coaching and mentoring at critical moments in their school life, which usually involves overcoming a learning barrier or extending a particular capability. Such schools have systematically reviewed the range of opportunities provided in this way as meeting every student's needs and demonstrating that every child matters. Such schools are also using workforce reform to create a more effective and extended use of learning assistants, integration assistants, literacy volunteers and language assistants, peripatetic music teaching and sports coaches, resident artists, peer tutors and a range of community and business volunteers, who can both coach and mentor. In doing this they make sure learning and educating is actually shared among all staff, not just the teachers. The more that can be done to target human resources onto the learning needs of individual students, in a context of a changing curriculum and school design and organization, the more likely it is we shall make a reality of our ambition that all children will succeed.

Unlocking staff energy

Another example of a critical intervention would be *unlocking the energy of all the staff* by making a determined effort to build a learning community through collective ownership and leadership, staff development and participation in innovation and action research. We know that the personal and professional growth of teachers is closely related to student growth, and creating time for staff to learn together will make performance more effective and consistent across the school.

Opportunities are needed to share inputs on subject specialisms and pedagogy, and for teachers and other staff in and beyond the school to work together across the curriculum to share good practice, hone their knowledge and skills, and develop their confidence in different ways of teaching and learning. Features of such an approach will be collective enquiry, peer observation and coaching, and shared learning. Everyone can make a difference to the craft knowledge of the school, and the trick is to capture contributions in the form of individual learning examples or annual learning plans, or by everybody being involved in a planned series of specific reviews critically evaluating current practices.

Widespread ownership of the improvement process is vital and sometimes this can be achieved by creating a 'school improvement group' with membership drawn from different levels in the school and reflecting a range of experience and perspectives across the whole staff team. The accreditation of learning, whether for parents, lunchtime supervisors, learning assistants, other school workers or teaching staff, often is a major feature of the school's provision. In the future, schools will be geared to innovation and research, with a commitment to publishing case studies and organizing an annual learning conference open to other schools and educationalists and, crucially, each school will be linked to other schools, higher education and the educational community as a whole, enabling it to learn its way forward.

Developing the student voice

A final example of a critical intervention would be the *development of the student voice*, and through that the promotion of a positive ethos. Both Howard Gardner in his work on 'Multiple Intelligences'[1] and Daniel Goleman in his book *Emotional Intelligence* have argued that the development of personal and interpersonal intelligences among children and young people is the most important element of any school's work.

A school could make a critical intervention around promoting particular competences in areas such as motivating oneself, knowing and managing emotions, and handling relationships, with the particular aim of building self-esteem, which in turn would drive improvement and achievement and enhance the school as a learning community. To do so would mean the adoption of specific strategies, such as circle time in primary schools or the positive use of tutor time in secondaries. At its heart would be a personal and social education programme; but to promote a positive ethos and to change the culture of the school significantly will involve teaching and learning strategies that encourage the development of emotional literacy, the full involvement of students in the life and work of the school, and the provision of a wide range of personalized learning opportunities.

Those schools that are seeking to make a significant step change in terms of improvement through deliberately targeting the raising of students' self-esteem will be aiming to provide openings for all students to be successful. This includes the proper recognition of a broad spectrum of achievement and giving all students the chance to accept responsibility and the support to carry it well. Particular practices would include the fostering of student responsibility and leadership, whether through Student Councils, the appointment of students to help

---

[1] H. Gardner, *The Unschooled Mind,* Basic Books (1995).

in the running of individual classes, or the general administration of the school community. Prefects are the obvious example (hopefully, interviewed appropriately with proper job descriptions and person specifications), but there can be a considerable range of opportunities – librarians, mentors, peer tutors, the running of clubs and societies, many involving training and accreditation. Some schools have developed 'hospitality teams' or 'young ambassadors' to take major responsibility for event-hosting duties at the school, from invitations to car-parking, welcoming and seating, or showing visitors around the school. Others have major 'community teams', who take particular interest in liaising with the local community and in some forms of community service.

There are other opportunities to build self-esteem and student leadership through the extended curriculum, such as Young Enterprise and Citizenship Schemes. A school intent in building self-esteem and promoting a positive ethos will strive to deliver, formally and informally, a programme of emotional literacy and to involve students significantly in the full life of the school. Students are partners in the school improvement process and can do much, if consulted appropriately, to develop this. Indeed, all improving schools involve students in decisions that affect them.

As we have previously remarked, the quality and range of small and large interventions and the extent of their leverage are crucial success factors in improving schools. Where there is a shared culture and understanding of the processes of improvement, a collective review process will provide the dynamic to succeed. When people truly share a vision they are connected, bound together by a common aspiration. Personal visions derive their power from an individual's deep caring for the vision. Shared visions derive their power from a common caring. In fact, we have come to believe that one of the reasons people seek to build shared visions is their desire to be connected in an important undertaking. Shared vision is vital for the learning organization because it provides the focus and energy for learning.

Quotations

Collective review is ensuring that the sum of the parts are exceeded by the collective whole.

Tim Brighouse and David Woods
How to Improve Your School

Sometimes when I consider what tremendous consequences come from little things … I am tempted to think … there are no little things.

Bruce Barton
Quoted in S.R. Covey
The Seven Habits of Highly Effective People

The silly question is the first intimation of some totally new development.

A.N. Whitehead
The Aims of Education and Other Essays

The art of progress is to preserve order amid change, and to preserve change amid order.

A.N. Whitehead
The Aims of Education and Other Essays

If you do not raise your eyes you will think you are at the highest point.

Antonia Porchia

If you would hit the mark, you must aim a little above it; Every arrow that flies feels the attraction of the earth.

Henry Longfellow
'Elegiac Verses'

Efficiency is concerned with doing things right. Effectiveness is doing the right things.

Peter F. Drucker
Post-Capitalist Society

Horse races and marathons, the difference is crucial. In a marathon everyone who finishes 'wins', the aim for nearly everyone is only to better their previous time. In a horse race the first three count and the rest are 'also rans'. We can organise both life and organisations so that they are marathons or horse races. It is largely a matter of choice. Competition, after all, is all around us. We cannot escape from competitors, but we can choose to see them as people who might beat us for the prize, or as fellow runners. It does not require much ingenuity to build in the kind of milestones and targets which marathon runners need. They all carry watches and have a well marked route to measure themselves against. They are running against themselves.

Charles B. Handy
Inside Organisations

The seat of knowledge is in the head; of wisdom, in the heart. We are sure to judge wrong if we do not feel right.

William Hazlitt

If one does not know to which port one is
sailing, no wind is favourable.

Seneca

Change comes from small initiatives which work,
initiatives which imitated, become the fashion.
We cannot wait for great visions from great
people, for they are in short supply at the end of
history. It is up to us to light our own small fires
in the darkness.

Charles B. Handy
The Empty Raincoat

Vision is an expression of a desirable direction
and destination for a school, underpinned by the
school's own philosophy. All those connected to
the school are able to articulate their values,
beliefs and aims and their attention is focused on
working towards a common ideal – vision bridges
the past, present and future of the school.

B. Nanus
Visionary Leadership

We need to prepare ourselves for the possibility that sometimes big changes follow from small events, and that sometimes these changes can happen very quickly.

Malcolm Gladwell
The Tipping Point

Change is the sum of a thousand acts of reperception and behaviour at every level of the organisation.

John J. Kao
Jamming: The art and discipline of business creativity

Where there is no vision, the people perish.

The Bible: Proverbs

Optimists underestimated the inequalities of the march, overplayed the benefits of business management technology, school-based management, market place competition … and misunderstood what good teaching demands.

D. Tyack and L. Cuban
Tinkering toward Utopia

Those who are going nowhere usually get there.

Anon

A school without a vision is a vacuum inviting intrusion.

Roland S. Barth
Improving Schools from Within

Not everything that can be counted counts and not everything that counts can be counted.

Albert Einstein
Out of My Later Years

The road to school improvement is always under construction.

Anon

Educational change depends on what teachers do and think – it's as simple and as complex as that.

Michael Fullan
The New Meaning of Educational Change

A school is four walls surrounding the future.

Roland S. Barth
Improving Schools from Within

In the varied topography of professional practice, there is a high, hard ground overlooking the swamp. On the high ground, manageable problems lead themselves to solutions through the application of research based theory and technique. In the swampy lowland, messy, confusing problems defy technical solutions.

D.A. Schonn
The Reflective Practitioner

Good schools face outwards as well as inwards, keeping their eye on the horizon as well as the bottom line.

D.H. Hargreaves
Creative Professionalism

Knowledge comes on the coat-tails of thinking. Instead of knowledge centred schools we need thinking centred schools.

David Perkins
Smart Schools

Re-culturing is the challenge of transforming mind-sets, visions, paradigms, images, metaphors, beliefs and shared meanings that sustain existing … relationships and of creating a detailed language and code of behaviour through which the desired new reality can be lived on a daily basis … It is about inventing what amounts to a new way of life.

G. Morgan
Images of Organization

In a learning community boundaries are pushed – inevitably this requires being open to new ideas, open to people who think outside the box, open to the 'mavericks' on the staff, open to divergent thinkers, able to live with uncertainty, willingness to take risks and make mistakes, but also having the confidence to keep going.

Stoll, Fink and Earl
It's About Learning and it's About Time

It is one of life's great ironies: schools are in the business of teaching and learning, yet they are terrible at learning from each other. If they ever discover how to do this their future is assured.

Michael Fullan
Change Forces: The Sequel

The intelligent school is greater than the sum of its parts. Through the use of its corporate intelligence it is in a powerful position to improve its effectiveness.

MacGilchrist, Myers and Reed
The Intelligent School

Learning disabilities are tragic in children but they are fatal in organisations.

Peter M. Senge
The Fifth Discipline

A whole school teaches in three ways:

By what it teaches
By how it teaches
By the kind of place it is

Anon

Let me be quite clear. The goal is system improvement … this means that a school head has to be almost as concerned about the success of other schools as he or she is about his or her own school. This is so because sustained improvement of schools is not possible unless the whole system is moving forward.

Michael Fullan
Leading in a Culture of Change

In schools, treading water is no longer an option. School people must either propel themselves in some direction, be towed, or sink.

Roland S. Barth
Improving Schools from Within

A learning organisation is an organisation that is continually expanding its capacity to create its future.

Peter M. Senge
The Fifth Discipline

I am prepared to go anywhere, provided it be forward.

David Livingstone

Schools are institutions in which the work is directed towards the future: they should have no place for someone who is pessimistic about it.

Bodil Jönsson
Ten Thoughts about Time

Trifles make perfection, but perfection is no trifle.

Italian proverb

The school reform movement has tended to operate on the false assumption that you could fix the schools so that the schools can fix the kids, no matter what the hell is happening in their families and communities.

Harold Howe II

Better schooling will result in the future – as it has in the past and does now – chiefly from the steady reflective efforts of the practitioners who work in schools and from the contributions of the parents and citizens who support (while they criticise) public education.

D. Tyack and L. Cuban
Tinkering toward Utopia

Remember that ...

Some people make things happen
Some people watch things happen
Some people wonder what happened

Anon

According to the theory of aerodynamics, the bumble-bee is unable to fly. This is because the size, weight, and shape of its body in relation to the total wing spread make flying impossible. But the bumble-bee, ignorant of these profound scientific truths, goes ahead and flies anyway and also manages to make a little honey every day.

Anon

You cannot achieve a new goal by applying the same level of thinking that got you where you are today.

Albert Einstein

Good is the enemy of great. We don't have great schools principally because we have good schools.

Jim Collins
Good to Great

If one of the fundamental purposes of schooling is pupil learning, the adults who work with pupils, whether directly or indirectly, must also learn. When flying we are told that if the air pressure drops, oxygen masks will appear and we must cover our own faces first before putting them on our children's faces. In schools, we are so busy stuffing the masks onto pupils' faces that we, ourselves, cannot breathe.

Roland S. Barth
Improving Schools from Within

When flying between the Earth and the Moon, the Apollo spacecraft were off course more than 90 per cent of the time. On their lunar voyages the crews would constantly bring the craft back to its intended trajectory. They were not on a perfect path but a critical path. Because they knew their intended target they could correct their spacecraft whenever it wandered off.

Anon

He has the right to criticise who has the heart to help.

Abraham Lincoln
Quoted in F. Sennett, *400 Quotable Quotes*
From the World's Leading Educators

School improvement is a journey where we travel as pilgrims not as nomads

Anon

Butterflies

School butterfly collections

Description

During a Teacher Day staff were divided into subject departments and were asked to discuss 'butterflies' – little things that they had done that had proved really effective.

Each department was then asked to write up five butterflies on a set pro forma, so they could create their own school 'Butterfly Book'. Another school publishes one butterfly per week in the staff bulletin, particularly on teaching and learning strategies. Other schools are beginning to create their own collections based on specific themes and issues.

Comment on impact

This is a very successful aid to staff development with high leverage in terms of managing change. It leads to an even greater sharing of ideas on school improvement and school effectiveness and demonstrates that the school is a research community, through publishing ideas that can improve teaching and learning.

Making walls talk

Description

Schools are looking for easy ways to improve the environment. One school decided through professional development and performance management interviews and a review of application forms to find out the private interests and hobbies of all staff. Discovering a keen amateur photographer among the technicians they commissioned her for a £500 sum and the cost of materials to take an extensive and representative range of photographs of school activities – lessons, playtimes, sports workshops, drama, music, lunchtimes and staff meetings. They then paid £500 to another support staff colleague to mount and display the results throughout the school. The total cost of the scheme – materials etc. – was £3,500 but the outcome is a much-appreciated exhibition of school and faculty life. The scheme is to be renewed each year.

A variation on this scheme would be to get students with similar hobbies to run the scheme – again suitably rewarded.

Comment on impact

The leadership team came up with this idea, but arranged for each faculty team to discuss it so that they could decide which area of display should be used, and whether the display could have a 'faculty' slant. This butterfly also puts one in mind of the sampler which Alec Clegg (former CEO of West Riding) said was on his aunt's wall:

> If thou of fortune be bereft
> And of thine earthly store have left
> Two loaves, sell one and with the dole
> Buy hyacinths to feed the soul.

The school in exploring its staff's private interests was keen to identify 'hyacinths'.

'Quid for a quote' – a cost-effective way of improving the environment

Description

The headteacher believed that pieces of prose and poetry as well as snappy epigrams and other quotations are often an opportunity to stir the mind of the passer-by into profitable thought. He discussed his idea of 'quid for a quote' at a staff meeting. It was adopted enthusiastically.

So at the start of the school year in each assembly the head of year and one of the school leadership team each did a piece about one of their favourite quotations. This was followed up in the tutor group. The first homework of term was for each student in the school to go home and discuss with the family or carer five favourite quotes. ('We chose five because we thought it would be OK.') Then on completion at least one from each student was simply framed and displayed, as for example:

> This is the true joy in life, being used for a purpose recognised by yourself as a mighty one; ... being part of a great enterprise rather than a feverish selfish little clod of ailments complaining that the world won't devote itself to making you happy ... I want to be thoroughly used up when I die, for the harder I work the more I live ... Life is no brief candle to me. It's a sort of splendid torch which I've got hold of for the moment and I want to make it burn as brightly as possible before handing it on to future generations.

George Bernard Shaw: *Man and Superman* (1903)
Presented by Jude Smith, Year 9

Then the school sent £1 home with the student for the parents to give to a charity of their choice.

Comment on impact
The visual, aural and behavioural impact of the school plays an important part in the likelihood of the school's success. Ensuring the visual environment is stimulating is always a problem. This scheme provided a simple way to raise awareness of the issue right across the school. (It is worth mentioning that the school in question is in a 'rotting' 1960s/70s building but internally is now a visual delight.)

Learning through action research and case studies

Description

A school decided to promote learning by 'action research'. All staff were invited to form into six groups to discuss case studies of success in the school. Each group identified possible topics and volunteers wrote the first refinements of practice that might transform something already good into something even better. An editorial group then worked on the text and the results were published as a school booklet.

The school feels that the case studies are good evidence of self-evaluation practice, and will commission further studies so as to be able to collect evidence on the way rather than retrospectively as preparation for an Ofsted inspection.

Comment on impact

The school chose an activity that was likely to increase the store of intellectual activity among the staff, believing that the process would release energy rather than consume it. It is very pleasing to have some rich case studies which celebrate their successes along the journey of school improvement.

Transforming attitudes towards achievement

Description

The headteacher was explaining to the assembled lower school the importance of effort and achievement. It was the beginning of a school year. 'When you look at your work in any subject, your teacher wants you to be making progress as well as consolidating what you know already. Of course, it's important to practise … but the real prize is when you make the next step forward in your skill, whether it is at sport, or in your understanding of academic work. But it is up to you to set targets for extending your skills in your subjects and, of course, your knowledge and understanding.' The headteacher then went on to explain how she and the three deputies would be helping children to do just that. At lower school assembly on Tuesdays, Wednesdays and Thursdays throughout the year the four of them would be giving the names of four youngsters who would then bring their books – all their books – to them at break times on that particular day. 'So it is important you think about where you are in your subjects, and that you pick out one thing which you are really proud of in your progress, and another you would like to improve on with help. A sort of obstacle you can tell us about.'

Of course the school accompanied this initiative with some careful planning among the tutors in Years 7, 8 and 9 and the year heads, so they too spent some time in tutorials, preparing youngsters for the sort of discussions they might have with the Senior Management Team.

Comment on impact

The virtues of this initiative include the head and the three deputies showing interest in 'teaching and learning'. It was also shared leadership because the suggestion for the move had come from their form tutors who wanted work on day books (of Records of Achievement) to be given higher profile. It is hard to escape the conclusion that the school's marking policy would be given greater emphasis. Indeed the Senior Management Team said it was a less threatening way of establishing an assessment consistency in that respect than the time-honoured one of heads calling in a whole class's examples of books and marking. Moreover, during the year the SMT would engage in meaningful conversations with 360 children in a lower school of 500. The school says it intends to keep it up to see if the outcomes at 16-plus will be affected. They believe they will. A further extension of the scheme was being considered – namely to send a personal letter, hand-written, to the parents of the particular children concerned to reinforce home–school partnerships.

Every quotation contributes something to the stability or enlargement of the language.

Samuel Johnson
Dictionary, 1775

It is a good thing to read books of quotations … the quotation when engraved upon the memory gives you good thoughts. They also make you anxious to read the authors and look for more.

Winston S. Churchill
My Early Life

Sources

Abbott, John (1994), *Learning makes Sense – Recreating education for a changing future*, Education 2000, Letchworth

Adams, Henry B. (1918), *The Education of Henry Adams*, Houghton Mifflin, Boston

Ayers, William (1993), *To Teach: The journey of a teacher*, Teacher's College Press, New York and London

Barber, Michael (1996), *The Learning Game: Arguments for an education revolution*, Victor Gollancz, London, a division of the Orion Publishing Group

Barth, Roland S. (1990), *Improving Schools from Within*, Jossey-Bass, San Francisco

Beare, H., B.J. Caldwell & R.H. Millikan (1989), *Creating an Excellent School*, Routledge, London

Beckett, Samuel (1983), *Wortsward Ho*, Calder, London

Beerbohm, Max (1946), *Mainly on the Air*, Heinemann, London

Blaikie, W.G. (1894), *The Personal Life of David Livingstone*, Murray, London

Blunkett, D. (2000), *Raising Aspirations in the 21st Century*, DfEE

Botts, Linda (1980), *Loose Talk*, Quick Fox/Rolling Stone Press, New York

Brighouse, Tim and David Woods (1999), *How to Improve Your School*, Routledge, London

Brighouse, Tim and David Woods (1999), *School Improvement Butterflies* (Birmingham), Questions Publications, Birmingham

Brighouse, Tim and David Woods (2005), *Butterflies for School Improvement*, DfES

Bronowski, Jacob (1973), *The Ascent of Man*, BBC, London

Carter, Hodding Jr, *A Collection of Poems*, Delpha Democratic Times, Greenville, MO

Casals, Pablo (1970), *Joys and Sorrows: Reflections*, MacDonald & Co., London

Chitty, Clive (2001), 'IQ, Racism and the Eugenics Movement', *Forum* 43

Churchill, W.S. (1937), *Great Contemporaries*, Thornton Butterworth. Reproduced with permission of Curtis Brown Ltd, London on behalf of The Estate of Winston Churchill. Copyright Winston S. Churchill

Churchill, W.S. (1943), *Onwards to Victory*, Cassell & Co., London. Reproduced with permission of Curtis Brown Ltd, London on behalf of The Estate of Winston Churchill. Copyright Winston S. Churchill

Churchill, W.S. (1944), *My Early Life*, Macmillan & Co., London. Reproduced with permission of Curtis Brown Ltd, London on behalf of The Estate of Winston Churchill. Copyright Winston S. Churchill

Clegg, Sir A. (1980), *About our Schools*, Blackwell, Oxford

Collins, Jim (2001), *Good to Great*, Random House, London

Connolly, K.J. (1999), 'In Praise of Difference', *Departmental Medicine and Child Neurology* 35 (11)

Covey, S.R. (1992), *The Seven Habits of Highly Effective People*, Simon & Schuster, New York

De Pree, Max (1992), *Leadership Jazz*, Doubleday, New York

Deming, W.E. (1989), *Out of the Crisis*, Cambridge University Press, Cambridge

Dewey, John (1916), *Democracy and Education: An introduction to the philosophy of education*, Macmillan, New York

Dictionary of Quotations (1987), Bloomsbury Publishing, London

Dixon, Peter (1988), *Grow your own Poems*, Macmillan Education, London

Doyle, W. (1990), 'Classroom Knowledge as a Foundation for Teaching', *Teachers College Record*

Drucker, Peter F. (1993), *Post-Capitalist Society*, Butterworth-Heinemann, Oxford. Reprinted with permission from Elsevier

Einstein, Albert (1935), *The World as I See It*, Bodley Head, London

Einstein, Albert (1950), *Out of My Later Years*, Thames & Hudson, London, with kind permission of Philosophical Library Inc. New York

Eisner, Elliot W. (1979) *The Educational Imagination*, Macmillan, New York

Eliot, T.S. (1939), *A Family Reunion: A Play*, Faber & Faber, London. Copyright 1939 by T.S. Eliot and renewed 1967 by Esme Valerie Eliot, reprinted by permission of Harcourt, Inc.

Everyman's Dictionary of Quotations and Proverbs (1952), ed. D.C. Browning, Dent, London

Freire, Paolo (1972), *Pedagogy of the Oppressed*, Sheed & Ward, London

Fried, Robert L. (1995), *The Passionate Teacher*. Copyright © by Robert L. Fried. Reprinted by permission of Beacon Press, Boston

Fullan, Michael (1991), *The New Meaning of Educational Change*, Cassell, London, a division of the Orion Publishing Group

Fullan, Michael (1993), *Change Forces: Probing the depths of education reform*, Falmer, London

Fullan, Michael (1999), *Change Forces: The Sequel*, Falmer, London

Fullan, Michael (2001), *Leading in a Culture of Change*, Jossey-Bass, San Francisco

Fullan, Michael (2003), *Change Forces with a Vengeance,* Routledge/Falmer, London

Fullan, Michael (2004), *The Moral Imperative of School Leadership*, Sage, London

Gardner, Howard (1991), *The Unschooled Mind: How children think and how schools should teach*, Basic Books, New York

Gardner, Howard (1995), *Leading Minds: Anatomy of leadership*, Basic Books, New York

Gibran, Kahlil (1931), *The Prophet*, Alfred A. Knopf, New York

Ginott, H.G. (1972), *Teacher and Child: A book for parents and teachers*, Macmillan, New York

Gladwell, Malcolm (2000), *The Tipping Point: How little things can make a difference*, Little Brown, London

Goleman, D. (1996), *Emotional Intelligence*, Bloomsbury, London

Gould, Stephen J. (1981), *The Mismeasure of Man*, Norton, New York and London. Copyright © 1981 by Stephen Jay Gould. Used by permission of W. W. Norton & Company, Inc.

Grey, D. (2005), *Grey's Essential Miscellany for Teachers*, Continuum Publishing, London

Handy, Charles B. (1990), *Inside Organisations*, BBC Books, London

Handy, Charles B. (1994), *The Empty Raincoat: Making sense of the future*, Hutchinson, London. Reprinted by permission of the Random House Group Ltd

Handy, Charles B. (1997), *The Hungry Spirit*, Hutchinson, London. Reprinted by permission of the Random House Group Ltd

Handy, Charles B. (1989), *The Age of Unreason*, Hutchinson Business, London. Reprinted by permission of the Random House Group Ltd

Hargreaves, A. (1993), *Changing Teachers, Changing Times*, Cassell, London, a division of the Orion Publishing Group

Hargreaves, A. and M. Fullan (1998), *What's Worth Fighting for in Education?*, Open University Press / McGraw-Hill Publishing Company. Reproduced by kind permission of the publisher

Hargreaves, D.H. (1982), *The Challenge for the Comprehensive School*, Routledge & Kegan Paul, London

Hargreaves, D.H. (1998), *Creative Professionalism*, Demos, London

Hargreaves, D.H. (2003), *Working Laterally: How innovation networks make an education epidemic*, DfES, Nottingham

Hart, S., A. Dixon, A.J. Drummond and D. McIntyre (2004), *Learning without Limits*, Open University Press / McGraw-Hill Publishing Company. Reproduced by kind permission of the publisher

Havel, Vaclav (1990), *Disturbing the Peace*, Faber, London

Hay McBer (2000), *Research into Teacher Effectiveness*, DfEE, Nottingham

Heaney, Seamus (1990), *The Cure at Troy*, Faber & Faber, London

Heubner, D., 'Religious Metaphors in the Language of Education', *Religious Education* 80 (3)

Highet, Gilbert (1950), *The Art of Teaching*, Alfred A. Knopf, New York

Hoffer, Eric (1998), *Vanguard Management*

Huberman, Michael (1992), 'Teacher Development and Instruction of Mastery' in Hargreaves & Fullan (eds), *Understanding Teacher Development*, Cassell, London

The Hutchinson Dictionary of Business Quotations (1996), comp. J. Cresswell and A. Leinster, Helicon, Oxford

Iacocca, Lee (1988), *Talking Straight*, Sidgwick and Jackson, London

The International Education Quotations Encyclopaedia (1995), ed. K.A. Noble, Open University Press, Buckingham

The International Thesaurus of Quotations (1978), ed. R.J. Tripp, Penguin, Harmondsworth

Johnson's Dictionary, A Modern Selection 2005, Dover Publications

Jönsson, B. (2003), *Ten Thoughts about Time: A philosophical enquiry*, Constable, London

Kao, John J. (1996), *Jamming: The art and discipline of business creativity*, HarperCollins, London

Kipling, R. (1893), *Many Inventions*, Macmillan & Co., London. Reprinted by permission of A P Watt Ltd on behalf of the National Trust for Places of Historic Interest or Natural Beauty

Kipling, R. (1902), *Just So Stories*, Macmillan & Co., London. Reprinted by permission of A P Watt Ltd on behalf of the National Trust for Places of Historic Interest or Natural Beauty

Kline, P. (1988), *The Everyday Genius*, Great Ocean Publishers, Arlington, VA

Kotter, J.P. (1990), 'What Leaders Really Do', *Harvard Business Review*

Lawrence, Elizabeth (1971), *Lob's Wood*, Cincinnati Nature Centre

Leese, J. (1950), *Personalities and Power in English Education*, Arnold, London

Little, Judith W. (1981), *The Power of Organisational Setting*, National Institute of Education, Washington DC

Locke, John (1693) Some *Thoughts Concerning Education*, ed. F.W. Garforth (1964), Heinemann, London

Louis, K.S and Miles, M.B. (1990), *Improving the Urban High School*, Teacher's College Press, New York and London

Lucas, B. (2005), *Discover your Hidden Talents*, Network Educational Press, Stafford

MacBeath, J. (1999), *Schools Must Speak for Themselves*, Routledge, London

MacGilchrist, B., Myers, K. and Reed J. (1997), *The Intelligent School*, Paul Chapman, London

Mandela, N. (1994), *Long Walk to Freedom*, Little Brown, London

McCourt, Frank (2005), *Teacher Man*, Fourth Estate, London. Reprinted by permission of HarperCollins Ltd. © Frank McCourt 2005

Mistral, Gabriela (2003), *Selected Poems*, trans. Ursula Le Guin, University of New Mexico Press

Montessori, M. (1949), *The Absorbent Mind*, Theosophical Publishing House, Madras

Morgan, G. (1986), *Images of Organization*, Sage, Beverly Hills and London

Morris, Estelle (2001), *Professionalism and Trust: The future of teachers and teaching*, DfES, Nottingham

Nanus, B. (1992), *Visionary Leadership*, Jossey-Bass, San Francisco

The New Penguin Dictionary of Modern Quotations (2000), ed. Robert Andrews, Penguin, London

The New Penguin Dictionary of Quotations (1991), ed. J.M. Cohen and M.J. Cohen, Penguin, London

Nicolson, Harold (1935), *Dwight Morrow*, Constable & Co., London

The Oxford Dictionary of Humorous Quotations (2001), ed. N. Sherwin, Oxford University Press, Oxford

The Oxford Dictionary of Phrase, Saying, and Quotation (2002), ed. Susan Ratcliffe, Oxford University Press, Oxford

The Oxford Dictionary of Quotations (2004), ed. E. Knowles, Oxford University Press, Oxford

Perkins, David (1992), *Smart Schools*, Free Press, New York and London

Piaget, J. (1952), *The Origins of Intelligence in Children*, International Universities Press, New York

Quotations for our Time (1978), ed. L.J. Peter, Souvenir Press, London

Rawls, J. (1971), *A Theory of Justice*, Harvard University Press, Cambridge, MA

Robinson, K. (2002), *Out of Our Minds: Learning to be creative*, Capstone, Oxford

Rogers, Carl and H.J. Freiberg (1983), *Freedom to Learn*, Merrill, Columbus and London

Rubin, Louis (1985), *Artistry in Teaching*, Random House, New York

Schonn, D.A. (1983), *The Reflective Practitioner*, Basic Books, New York

Senge, Peter M. (1990), *The Fifth Discipline: The art and practice of the learning organisation*, Doubleday, New York

Sennett, F. (2004), *400 Quotable Quotes from the World's Leading Educators*, Corwin Press, Sage, Thousand Oaks, CA and London

Sergiovanni, T.J. (2001), *Leadership: What's in it for schools?*, Routledge/Falmer, London

Skinner, B.F. (1964), *New Scientist*, 21 May 1964

Smith, Jonathan (2000), *The Learning Game: A teacher's inspirational story*, Little Brown, London

Spark, M. (1961), *The Prime of Miss Jean Brodie*, Macmillan, London

Stoll, Clifford (1995), *Silicon Snake Oil*, Doubleday, London and New York

Stoll, L., D. Fink and L. Earl (2003), *It's About Learning and it's About Time*, Routledge/Falmer, London

Ted Wragg: A Tribute (2006), Times Educational Supplement/Routledge

Temple, W. (1941), *Citizen and Churchman*, Eyre & Spottiswoode, London

Thring, Edward (1883), *Theory and Practice of Teaching*, Cambridge University Press, Cambridge

Toffler, A. (1990), *Powershift*, Bantam Books, New York and London

Toffler, A. (1998), *Information Studies*, Toronto

Tyack, David (1974), *The One Best System: A history of American urban education*, Harvard University Press, Cambridge, MA. Reprinted by permission of the publisher, copyright © 1974 by the President and Fellows of Harvard College

Tyack, D. and L. Cuban (1995), *Tinkering toward Utopia: A century of public school reform*, Harvard University Press, Cambridge, MA. Reprinted by permission of the publisher, copyright © 1974 by the President and Fellows of Harvard College

Van Maurik, J. (2001), *Writers on Leadership*, Penguin Business

Wells, H.G. (1920), *The Outline of History*, Macmillan, New York. Reprinted by permission of A P Watt Ltd on behalf of The Trustees of GP Wells

White, M.A. (1971), in *The Experience of Schooling*, ed. M.A. White and M.L. Silberman. © 1971. Reprinted with permission of Wadsworth, a division of Thomson Learning: www.thomson.rights.com. Fax 800 730-2215

Whitehead, A.N. (1932), *The Aims of Education and Other Essays*, Macmillan, New York

Williams, Carol (1998), *Bringing a Garden to Life*, Bantam Books, New York

Winterrowd, Wayne (1996), *Annuals for Connoisseurs*, Macmillan, London

Wragg, E.C. (2005), *The Art and Science of Teaching and Learning: The selected works of Ted Wragg*, Routledge, London

Previous publications by the authors

Brighouse, T., *What Makes A Good School?,* Network Educational Press, 1991

Woods, D.C. and S. Orlik, *School Review and Inspection*, Kogan Page, 1994

Brighouse, T. and D.C. Woods, *How to Improve Your School*, Routledge, 1999

Brighouse, T. and D.C. Woods, *School Improvement Butterflies (Birmingham)*, Questions Publications, Birmingham, 1999

Cribb, M. and D.C. Woods, *Effective LEAs and School Improvement*, Routledge Falmer, 2001

Brighouse, T. and D.C. Woods, B*utterflies for School Improvement (London Challenge)*, DfES, 2005

Brighouse, T., *Essential Pieces: The jigsaw of a successful school*, Research Machines Booklet, 2006

Network Continuum Education

We are delighted to present a truly inspired selection of new books from Network Continuum Education:

- **Pocket PALs** – a sensational new series of highly accessible pocket-sized books that have been perfectly designed to aid practical learning.

- **Homo Zappiens** – examines the effect of technology on children growing up in the digital age and shows how some schools are dramatically reshaping the learning experience to support our new generation of learners.

  ISBN-10: 185539 220 8   ISBN-13: 978 185539 220 5

- **Breaking through Barriers to Boys' Achievement** – a groundbreaking book by an exciting author that examines exactly why boys underachieve at school and the strategies that can be used to overcome the barriers to their learning.

  ISBN-10: 185539 211 9   ISBN-13: 978 185539 211 3

- **Helping Children with Yoga** – research shows that yoga can have really positive effects on children's learning and general well-being. This book shows how yoga postures and techniques can be used both safely and simply to benefit your children.

  ISBN-10: 185539 215 1   ISBN-13: 978 185539 215 1

- **Learning to Learn for Life 2** – Continuing the Learning to Learn for Life series, this is the second book of school-based examples for KS2 from the Campaign for Learning.

  ISBN-10: 185539 209 7   ISBN-13: 978 185539 209 0

- **Help Your Young Child to Succeed** – the follow-up to the popularly acclaimed Help Your Child to Succeed provides parents of 3–5 year olds with a definitive resource for giving their children the best start in life and preparing them for formal education.

  ISBN-10: 185539 214 3   ISBN-13: 978 185539 214 4

www.networkcontinuum.co.uk